CHANGE YOUR THINKING, CHANGE YOUR LIFE

SUCCESS *for* YOUNG ADULTS THROUGH *the* POWER *of* *the* SUBCONSCIOUS MIND

DR. JOSEPH MURPHY

MEDIA

Published 2023 by Gildan Media LLC
aka G&D Media
www.GandDmedia.com

CHANGE YOUR THINKING, CHANGE YOUR LIFE. Copyright ©2023 by Joseph Murphy
Trust. All rights exclusively licensed by JMW Group Inc., jmwgroup@jmwgroup.net.

Front Cover design by Tom Mckeveny

Interior design by Meghan Day Healey of Story Horse, LLC

Library of Congress Cataloging-in-Publication Data is available upon request

ISBN: 978-1-7225-0603-2

10 9 8 7 6 5 4 3 2 1

CONTENTS

PREFACE 9

How This Book Will Transform Your Life

Why Life Seems Unfair 9

Everybody Speaks to a Greater
Consciousness 11

A Practical Approach 12

Desire Is Affirmative Thought 13

Unlock Your Incredible Human
Potential 13

INTRODUCTION 15

ABOUT THIS BOOK 21

CHAPTER 1 23

Consciousness—Your Key to Limitless Power

What Is Consciousness? 23

Consciousness Experiments 25

What Is Subconsciousness? 27

What Is the Mind? 29

Conscious versus Subconscious
Mind 31

CHAPTER 2 33

Unleash Your Mind Power

How Your Mind Works 34

Planting Seeds of Thought 35

One Mind, Two Functions 37

Hypnosis Reveals the Subconscious
Mind in Action 38

Your Subconscious Does What It's
Told 39

CHAPTER 3 41

Tell Your Subconscious Mind What to Do: Affirmation and Other Techniques

Autosuggestion 43

Affirmation 44

The Art and Science of Affirmation 45

Problem Solving 47

Self-Hypnosis 48

Passing Over 49

Visualization 51

Dream Boards or Vision Boards 53

Mental Movie 54

Mantra 56

The Sleeping Technique 58

The "Thank-You" Approach   59

Feel the Love   61

Issuing a Directive   62

Acting As If   63

The Argumentative Method   64

Prayer   65

CHAPTER 4   67

Mind Power in Action— Real-Life Stories

A Dream Come True   67

The Shoulder Bag   68

Overcoming Stage Fright   69

Becoming a Doctor   70

Overcoming a Nasty Temper   71

Restored Vision   72

The Pharmacist   73

Nikola Tesla   75

He Fired Himself   76

Fear of Failure Conquered   76

All She Wanted Was a Sewing
     Machine   77

CHAPTER 5   79

Repair the Damage: Overcome Self-Limiting Thoughts Implanted in Your Mind

Heterosuggestion   80

Negative Self-Talk   81

Take Inventory   82

Reprogram Your Mind   84

The Power of an Assumed Major
     Premise   86

CHAPTER 6   89

Get Healthy and Fit

Give Your Body What It Needs   90

Focus on Health, Not Illness   92

One Universal Healing Principle   93

Unload Your Emotional Baggage   95

How I Healed Myself   98

Stories of Transformation   100

Your Story   100

CHAPTER 7   101

Make Lots of Money

Money Is a Mental Construct   102

Think Rich, Be Rich   102

Why Most People Lack Money   103

Hard Work Is Not Required   105

Don't Envy What Others Have   106

Money and a Balanced Life   106

Developing the Right Attitude Toward
     Money   108

How to Earn More Money at Work   108

Protect Your Investments   110

You Can't Get Something for
     Nothing   110

Your Constant Supply of Money   111

CHAPTER 8   113

Be Confident: Overcome Shyness and Fear

Overcoming Fear of Speaking in
     Public   114

Your Greatest Foe   115

Good Fear, Bad Fear   115

Document Your Fears   116

Challenge Your Fear's Trigger   118

Do What You Fear   120

Fear of Failure   121

Fear of Water   122

Using Your Imagination to Overcome
    Fear   123

Overcoming the Fear of Riding in an
    Elevator   124

Catastrophizing   125

De-Catastrophizing   126

Stare Down Your Fears   127

From Fear to Desire   128

They Plotted Against Him   129

Overcome Your Fear   129

CHAPTER 9   131

Excel at School and Work

From Failing Grades to Straight
    As   133

Define Success   134

The Three Steps to Success   135

True Success   139

Consult Your Board of Directors   141

Making "Success" Your Mantra   142

CHAPTER 10   143

Get Others to Respect You

Build Positive Self-Esteem   144

Be Assertive   145

Be Open-Minded   147

Resolve Disagreements Rationally   148

Resist Peer Pressure   149

Accept Criticism Gracefully   150

Embrace Your Vulnerability   151

Make Improvements, Not Excuses   153

CHAPTER 11   155

Make Friends and Nurture Friendships

Know What You Want in a Friend   156

Engage Your Subconscious Mind in
    Your Search   156

Make Friendship a Priority   157

Make Yourself an Attractive
    Target   158

Forgive   159

Put Yourself Out There   161

Initiate Contact   163

The Only Way to Have a Friend Is to
    Be One   163

Be Selective   165

CHAPTER 12   167

Find Your Soulmate

The Meaning of Intimacy   168

Imagine Your Soulmate   169

Attract Your Ideal Partner   169

No Need for a Third Mistake   171

Knowing When to End a
    Relationship   173

Drifting into a Breakup   174

The Emotionally Needy Partner   175

The Brooding Partner   176

Avoid the Big Mistake   177

Don't Try to Remake Your
    Partner   177

Four Steps to Harmonious
    Companionship   178

CHAPTER 13 181

Have More Fun

What's Your Idea of Fun? 182

Impress Your Idea of Fun on Your
Subconscious Mind 183

Make Dull Activities More Fun 184

Fill Your Mind with Smiles and
Laughter 186

CHAPTER 14 189

Travel the World

Choose a Destination 190

Get Your Mind in the Game 192

Explore Your Hometown and
Country 194

CHAPTER 15 197

Excel at School and Beyond

They Said I'd Never Amount to
Anything 198

Self-Motivate for Success in
School 199

What Do You Want to Learn
Next? 200

Trust Your Subconscious Mind to
Guide You 201

Ease into It 201

Sleep on It 203

Support Your Brain's Health and
Function 203

CHAPTER 16 205

Make the World a Better Place

Look for Trouble 206

Engage Your Imagination 207

Volunteer for a Cause 208

Meditate 209

Be Generous and Compassionate 211

CHAPTER 17 213

Develop Your Psychic Powers

Recognizing Different Psychic
Powers 214

You Are Psychic 216

She Sensed Danger 217

This Doctor Visited Patients with His
Astral Body 218

Everything He Needed Came His
Way 219

An Army Officer Hears His Brother's
Voice: "You Will Be Saved" 220

An Out-of-Body Experience 221

Fearlessly Experience This Awesome
Universe 222

NEXT STEPS 225

ABOUT THE AUTHOR 227

PREFACE

How This Book Will Transform Your Life

People from all walks of life experience health, wealth, happiness, and fulfillment. You can, too, when you start to tap the awesome power of your subconscious mind. As this book reveals, your mindset and mental imagery define your reality. As you think, so you are. This book guides you through the process of taking control of your conscious and subconscious thoughts, thereby empowering you to mold a reality of perfect health, wealth, happiness, and fulfillment.

Why Life Seems Unfair

Why is one person sad and another person happy? Why is one person joyful and prosperous while another is miserable and poor? Why is one person fearful and anxious and another full of faith and confidence? Why does one person have a beautiful, luxurious home while another is homeless? Why does one person succeed while others fail? Why is one teacher outstanding and immensely popular and another mediocre and unpopular? Why is one person a genius while others never come up with a creative or clever idea no matter how hard they try? Why is one person healed of a serious illness and another isn't? Why do so many kind, generous people suffer while many selfish, immoral people succeed and prosper? Why is one person happy in his or her romantic relationship, and another person unhappy and frustrated? Are there answers to these questions in the workings of your conscious and subconscious minds? There most certainly are.

Questions like these motivated the writing of this book. Its author, Dr. Joseph Murphy, asked the same questions, which all really boil down to a single question: Why does life seem so unfair?

To answer this question, he studied people throughout history, from ancient times to his contemporaries, and he studied the wisdom of the ages. The answer he found was simple—the happiest, healthiest, and most successful people in life were those who had discovered how to use the power of their subconscious mind to their advantage. They had a strong desire for something, they passed the idea to their subconscious mind fully convinced that their desire would be granted, and their subconscious mind delivered the solution. Yes, it's *that* simple.

This book reveals the great, fundamental truths about the human mind in plain and simple language. And it presents practical techniques for fully engaging your conscious and subconscious mind in the pursuit of health, wealth, happiness, and fulfillment. As you incorporate what you learn from this book into your life, you will begin to discover an overwhelming power within and beyond you that will lift you up from confusion, sadness, and disappointment and solve your difficulties. It will release you from emotional and physical distress and place you on the road to freedom, happiness, and peace of mind.

The power of your subconscious mind will replace scarcity with abundance, sickness with health, and sadness with joy. It will open the prison doors of fear and doubt to a confident future of limitless opportunity.

Everybody Speaks to a Greater Consciousness

Throughout the day, you speak to a greater consciousness. We all do. On a cold winter morning, as you approach your car, you may think, "I hope it starts today!" As you train for an athletic event, you may think about achieving your personal best or crushing your opponents. As you sit at your desk to take a final exam, you may be confident that you'll ace it or worry that you'll fail because you didn't prepare as you should have.

Where do you think all these thoughts go? They don't just flow through your mind. They enter the greater consciousness—the collective, universal consciousness that permeates everything and gives form to all energy and matter.

If your thoughts are peaceful, wholesome, and positive, you will be rewarded with health, prosperity, and happiness. Likewise, if your thoughts are dark and chaotic, full of fear and worry, they will be reflected in your circumstances. The purpose of this book is to encourage and empower you to communicate to the greater consciousness orderly, purposeful thoughts instead of the random, self-defeating thoughts that many of us are afflicted with.

Do you know how to communicate effectively with the greater consciousness? Religious people may pray to a higher being. Life coaches often recommend repeating daily affirmations. Some people simply commit to thinking positively and avoiding anything negative in their lives. These approaches are all effective to some degree for communicating with the greater consciousness, but having the right mindset is key. Merely hoping something good happens or repeating a prayer without thought or conviction will not deliver the desired results.

Psychologist and New Thought minister, Joseph Murphy studied the various approaches to prayer and to communicating with the greater consciousness. He then developed his own practical approach, which engages both the conscious and subconscious mind. He practiced this approach throughout his life to benefit himself and others. He cured illness, repaired broken relationships, helped people achieve prosperity, and even developed his own psychic powers—including mental telepathy (communicating with someone else solely through thought), clairvoyance (seeing into the future), and astral projection (visiting a place without physically traveling there). Dr. Murphy's approach to communicating with the cosmic consciousness is an easy formula to follow—a simple, repeatable pattern that delivers consistent results.

A Practical Approach

A unique feature of this book is its down-to-earth practicality. Here you are presented with simple, easy-to-use techniques and formulas that you can apply in your everyday experience. These simple processes have been taught to people all over the world. Part of this book's practical nature is the fact that it shows you not only how to get what you want, but also why you sometimes get the opposite of what you want.

People often ask, "Why is it I have prayed and prayed and gotten no answer? Why aren't my affirmations working?" In this book you will find the reasons for this common complaint.

Prayer, affirmation, and positive thinking alone are not enough. The missing ingredient is confidence (certainty). Any doubt, worry, or fear not only weakens your resolve and determination but also sends a mixed message to the greater consciousness that you're unclear about what you want.

Greater consciousness is the infinite intelligence that permeates everything. It is the matrix (framework) that gives form to energy and matter. Clarity and certainty of thought are what enable you to form your own reality through the power of your subconscious mind.

The law of life is the law of certitude. As you think, feel, and are certain it will be, so is the condition of your mind, body, and circumstances. A technique, a methodology based on an understanding of what you're doing and why you're doing it will empower you to subconsciously bring about the embodiment of all the good things in life. Essentially, effective communication with the greater consciousness is the key to unlocking the realization of your heart's desire.

Desire Is Affirmative Thought

Everyone wants health, happiness, security, peace of mind, acceptance, and love, but many fail to achieve clearly defined results. A university professor admitted, "I know that if I changed my mental pattern and redirected my emotional life, my headaches would clear up, but I don't have any technique or process to use. My mind wanders back and forth to my many problems, and I feel frustrated, defeated, and unhappy."

This professor had a desire for perfect health, but he lacked a clear and simple method for controlling his thoughts. By practicing the healing methods outlined in this book, he trained his mind to accept perfect health, and his headaches went away.

Unlock Your Incredible Human Potential

The power of your subconscious mind and cosmic consciousness are rooted in science, not religion. You don't need to adhere to any religion, philosophy, or system of belief. The physical and spiritual laws on which these powers are based are eternal and universal. They existed long before you were born, before religions came into existence, before our world existed. They require no special abilities. The power is unlimited and available to anyone who claims it.

This awesome, transformative power will rid you of mental and physical wounds, eliminate fears, and free you completely from the limitations of poverty, disappointment, and frustration. All you need to do is unite mentally and emotionally with the reality you envision for yourself, and the creative powers of your subconscious will respond accordingly. Begin now, today, and let wonders happen in your life.

INTRODUCTION

What if I were to tell you that you can be, do, and have nearly anything you desire strongly enough? You can be anything you want to be, do anything you want to do, have anything you want, and travel instantly, at the speed of thought, to any destination anywhere in the universe. What if I told you that you have psychic powers and the power to perform what most people would perceive as miracles?

You would probably think I was deranged. Maybe a religious fanatic.

But the fact is, thanks to the power of your subconscious mind, you can be, do, and have nearly anything you want and are bold enough to claim. You can heal yourself and others. You can communicate telepathically with others anywhere in the world. You can see into the future. You can perform miracles.

That would be awesome, wouldn't it?

People throughout the course of history have done it. You can too. In fact, you probably know people who have done it—phenomenally successful people who seem to accomplish whatever they put their mind to and get whatever they want. And they make it look easy. You wonder how they do it. If you asked them, they probably couldn't tell you. They may not know. It's just that they always expect the best, and that's what they get.

At the other end of the spectrum are the unfortunates who fail at nearly everything and rarely, if ever, get what they want. They believe that they're "victims of circumstance" and "never get a break." They're always in the wrong place at the wrong time. Life is always a struggle. They've come to accept and even expect the worst, and that's what they get. "It is what it is," right?

It's not entirely their fault. We've all been indoctrinated—we've had beliefs (some true, some not), values (some good, some bad), and even desires (what we want in life) ingrained in us—taught and modeled by others and molded by the media—books, magazines, movies, TV shows, advertisements, social media, and the list goes on.

To a large extent, we are products of the culture in which we've been raised, and from the day we're born, we're bombarded with negative, self-limiting thoughts (ideas that hold you back). To find out just how much you've been programmed to think negatively, read through the following statements to see how many of them you have ever said out loud or repeated in your mind:

- Money is the root of all evil.
- The rich get richer, and the poor get poorer.
- I can't afford it.
- I'm not _____ enough to _____.
- I'm too _____ to _____.
- It's not what you know but who you know.
- What's the use?
- I can't _____.
- Things are getting worse and worse.
- It's just a pipe dream. It'll never happen.

- You can't trust a soul.
- I haven't got a chance.
- There's no point in trying.
- Nice people finish last.
- Nothing worth having comes easy.
- I'm powerless to do anything about it.
- Nothing ever goes my way.
- Life sucks and then you die.
- It is what it is.
- Whatever . . .

If you marked more than a few statements in the list, you're probably being held back by limiting or self-defeating thoughts that have been programmed into you since birth. Worse yet, they may have become more deeply ingrained through experiences and observations. For example, if you've attempted and failed to achieve a certain goal several times in the past, you may take that as proof that "the cards are stacked against you"—that circumstances have prevented you from getting what you wanted.

It's time to reverse that thinking and take control of your life. It's not circumstances that form your thoughts, but thoughts that create your circumstances. Thanks to the power of your subconscious mind, which you can direct through your conscious thoughts, you can create your own reality—a beautiful, limitless reality.

Conscious desires conveyed to the subconscious mind with sufficient conviction or intent are carried out by the subconscious mind. For example, on a very basic level, your conscious mind issues a command to walk across the room, and your subconscious mind moves your limbs accordingly without any conscious effort on your part. On a higher level, if your conscious mind wants anything strongly enough to transfer that desire to your subconscious mind, your subconscious mind will find a way to make it happen. It will attract all the energy, determination, people, money, and other resources necessary.

The same concept applies to negative thoughts. If you've been led to believe that you'll never amount to anything, and that thought makes its way to your subconscious mind, then your subconscious mind will find ways to undermine your success. To paraphrase Henry Ford, Whether you believe you can or believe you can't, you're right. If you doubt your ability, you cannot succeed. Your subconscious acceptance of failure will undermine your efforts.

Your mind, thoughts, behaviors, and choices are the keys to your freedom and the keys to overcoming any obstacles that may be standing in your way. Your subconscious mind is connected to universal, collective consciousness, which permeates everything—all energy and matter, all things, all beings. As a result, whatever you think or desire with a strong enough conviction or intent, your subconscious mind, through universal consciousness, makes happen in the physical world.

This book reveals the power of the subconscious mind and delivers a no-nonsense program that will teach you how to think your way to getting what you want in life. You'll discover how you can be, do, or have whatever you are bold enough to claim. You will develop a positive, determined mindset along with techniques that enable you to use your conscious mind to plant thoughts in the fertile ground of your subconscious mind like the seeds of an abundant harvest.

Over time, as you experience higher and higher levels of success, your doubts and fears will vanish, and you will emerge as a more confident and creative version of yourself—the true version of yourself before your mind accepted the popular misconceptions of lack and limitation. Whatever idea or belief is dominant in your subconscious mind takes control of your thoughts and behaviors, which are responsible for the circumstances you encounter.

This book will transform your mindset. All day, every day you will claim the abundance you deserve, expect the best from yourself and others, and look forward with grateful anticipation to an awesome and limitless future. Gradually, your subconscious mind will align with this new, positive mindset and empower you to experience the joy, thrill, and fulfillment of your dreams.

The moment you change your conscious mind and begin to claim the good things of life—health, wealth, loving relationships, and more—your subconscious mind gets to work, making it your reality. When you take control of your thoughts, feelings, behaviors, and choices, you become at one with universal consciousness, which brings all things into being. When you master the practical skills and techniques presented in this book, you will begin to experience true freedom. You will no longer feel like a victim of circumstances as you become the creator and director of your life.

Nothing in this book is secret or new. The truths it reveals are universal and timeless, and the techniques have been in practice over the course of recorded human history. Many of the most successful and renowned individuals throughout history have tapped into the power of universal consciousness to fuel their accomplishments—religious leaders, mystics, writers, artists, musicians, inventors, architects, and even star athletes. Anyone who has experienced being "in the zone" and who has acted free of doubt, fear, or limitation to perform an incredible feat or to create or build something remarkable has benefited from the power of their subconscious mind.

Now, it's your turn. In this book, you will discover how to

- Use your conscious mind to program your subconscious mind to obtain or achieve whatever you desire,
- Overcome fear, doubt, and worry,
- Transform negative thoughts into their positive equivalents,
- Maintain peaceful, loving, productive relationships,
- Use your mind to heal your body and achieve your fitness goals,
- Achieve your full potential,
- Enjoy life more fully, and
- Become sensitive to your psychic abilities and begin to develop those abilities.

Reading this book will motivate you and teach you how to change your life for the better, but it won't, and it can't, accomplish this goal unless you put this guidance into practice in your life today, tomorrow, and every day from now on. In some ways, it's easy—change your thoughts, change your life. But changing deeply ingrained thinking and behavioral patterns requires time, effort, and persistence. Rest assured, the benefits far outweigh the investment. Your life will be totally transformed, and you will experience abundance that, right now, you probably can't even imagine.

Keep in mind that whatever your subconscious mind accepts as true has an impact on the physical world. A positive mindset creates positive energy that attracts positive people and ensures positive outcomes. A negative mindset destines you to a life of scarcity, frustration, and disappointment. You are the master of your own destiny. You have the power to think for yourself and the power to choose. Choose life! Choose love! Choose health! Choose happiness!

ABOUT THIS BOOK

This book is based on the teachings of Dr. Joseph Murphy as presented in his classic bestseller *The Power of Your Subconscious Mind*, which was first published in 1963. In fact, much of the content of this book is directly from Murphy's classic. We, the editorial team, updated the text to give it a more modern feel and modified it slightly to make it more relevant and appealing to a younger audience. We also wove practical exercises throughout the book to deliver a more interactive learning experience and simplify the process of putting Murphy's teachings into practice.

Murphy's wisdom and guidance are as relevant now as they were sixty years ago. More and more people are coming to realize that they are the authors of their own reality and that everything they create and achieve begins with a thought—that their power to change their lives begins with the power to change their minds. Science is adding to our understanding as researchers reveal more about the connections between the physical and metaphysical universe, between the natural and supernatural, and between mind and body.

We created this book to bring Dr. Murphy's teachings to a younger generation of readers—an audience that is perhaps more receptive to his ideas and where these ideas, when put into practice, can have the most transformative impact.

When your parents and teachers advise you to have confidence in yourself, when they tell you that you can achieve anything that you put your mind to, they are correct. However, they often fall short in explaining how this is possible and, more importantly, how to put their advice into practice. This book hands you the keys to unlock these mysteries.

CHAPTER 1

Consciousness— Your Key to Limitless Power

The universe looks less like a big machine
than a big thought.

—Dean Radin, Chief Scientist, Institute of Noetic Science

To begin to understand and appreciate the power of the subconscious mind, we first need to be clear about what consciousness, subconsciousness, and the mind are. Each of these words has multiple dictionary definitions along with numerous functional definitions (meanings specific to the context in which they're used).

In this chapter, you explore the different meanings of these words and the concepts they describe and begin to understand and appreciate your ability to use your mind to tap into the limitless power of the universe.

What Is Consciousness?

Most dictionary definitions of consciousness equate it with *awareness*. Here are a few definitions of consciousness from *Webster's Collegiate Dictionary* (11th edition):

- The quality or state of being aware, especially of something within oneself
- The state of being characterized by sensation, emotion, volition, and thought
- The totality of conscious states of an individual
- The normal state of conscious life
- The upper level of mental life of which the person is aware as contrasted with unconscious processes

These definitions lean toward what could be described as individual consciousness or self-consciousness—an awareness of one's own existence. It is the opposite of unconsciousness—being unaware of your own existence.

This book has a much more expansive definition of *consciousness* than what you'll find in any dictionary: Consciousness is the singular intelligence that permeates everything.

This expands the definition of consciousness in two ways:

- First, this more expansive definition of consciousness positions it within and beyond the individual. It exists regardless of whether you're conscious, regardless of whether you or anything else exists. The human mind has a faculty for experiencing consciousness, but consciousness is not confined within the human body or brain. It transcends and extends beyond the individual. Consciousness is the intelligence responsible for creation.
- Second, consciousness is awareness not merely in a passive, observational way, but also in an active, participatory way. For example, when you want something or you love someone or you imagine something, your consciousness is actively engaged. Regardless of whether you physically act on your thought or

emotion, your intent becomes part of consciousness and thereby it becomes part of the intelligence responsible for creation.

Think of consciousness as the Force in *Star Wars*—the mysterious energy that binds the galaxy together. In *Star Wars,* the Jedi and others who can harness the Force have special abilities such as mental telepathy, levitation, and astral projection. They also receive guidance from the Force. Through conscious intent, we, too, can direct the Force and open our minds to its infinite intelligence and wisdom. We have not only conscious awareness of the physical world but also the power to shape it.

Consciousness Experiments

The idea that we have the power, through conscious intent, to shape the physical world and what happens in that world has been put to the test. Scientists and engineers have conducted several experiments and studies to examine the impact of consciousness on the physical world.

In the late 1970s, Princeton University Professor Robert Jahn placed study participants near a random number generator and instructed them to try with their minds to influence the frequency of a certain number. This device would generate 0s and 1s randomly, like flipping a coin for heads or tails. Normally, over time, the device would generate a nearly equal number of 0s and 1s. However, during the study, in most cases, participants were able to use the power of their minds to increase the frequency of the number on which they concentrated. In other words, through conscious intent alone, participants could influence the output of an electronic device.

Building on Dr. Jahn's work, another Princeton professor, Roger Nelson, linked forty random number generators from all over the world to his Princeton laboratory. Normally, when results from the random number generators were tabulated and graphed, they formed a flat line indicating a nearly equal number of 0s and 1s. However, significant deviations from the expected norm were observed before and after many dramatic global events, including the funeral of Princess Diana and the 9/11 terrorist attacks.

Clearly, whatever people were thinking and feeling before, during, and shortly after these events generated sufficient energy to influence the output of these random number generators. The Global Consciousness Project now collects and examines data from more than seventy random number generators around the world. To learn more about this fascinating project, visit noosphere.princeton.edu.

In an experiment conducted at the Princeton Engineering Anomalies Research (PEAR) Lab, scientists constructed a dark room with a grow light positioned in the center of the ceiling. The light was controlled by a random number generator that could change its direction to illuminate different quadrants of the room. They placed a plant in a far corner of the room. Normally, with no plant in the room, the light would be distributed evenly around the four quadrants of the room. With the plant in a corner of the room, significantly more light shined in that corner.

Describing the results of the experiment, Adam Michael Curry, a leader in the consciousness research community, explained, "It's as though life itself, even life or consciousness in something as simple as a houseplant, bends probabilities in the physical world in the direction of what it needs, in the direction of its growth and its evolution."

Japanese researcher Masaru Emoto conducted experiments to study the impact of human consciousness on the crystalline structure of water. When water was exposed to positive, orderly thoughts and emotions, it formed beautiful, intricate crystals when frozen. When the same water was exposed to negative, chaotic thoughts and emotions, the frozen crystals were broken, misshapen, and discolored.

In another study, groups of trained meditators, equivalent in number to 1 percent of the population, were sent into communities to engage in periods of deep meditation. For example, 2,000 meditators would be sent into a town of 200,000 people. With the addition of trained meditators, these communities consistently experienced reductions in emergency room visits, violent crimes, robberies, and all kinds of negative behaviors, even though 99 percent of the population was totally unaware of the 1 percent engaged in meditation.

Results of these experiments and studies suggest that consciousness is pervasive and that it has the power to influence the physical word. As Curry said, "Consciousness does not seem to be strictly produced by the brain. It involves the brain, but there's something much deeper going on here. Consciousness may not be localized to our bodies but may be a fundamental feature of the physical world in which we live."

Physicist David Bohm concurs: "In this flow, mind and matter are not separate substances. Rather, they are different aspects of one whole and unbroken movement."

Curry concludes, "The Force is real."

What Is Subconsciousness?

Subconsciousness is generally defined as any mental process free of awareness or intent. Your subconscious mind is highly active 24/7 and is responsible for keeping you alive and healthy in this physical world. It controls all your life systems—respiration, circulation, digestion, immunity, and so on. It controls growth and reproduction. It repairs and restores the body after injury and illness. It also functions as the library of your mind, storing everything you've ever learned, perceived, and experienced.

In this book, the terms *conscious* and *subconscious* are used primarily to distinguish between conscious and subconscious minds and processes:

- The conscious mind controls all intentional body movement and engages in organized, logical, intentional thought.
- The subconscious mind controls all autonomous bodily functions and engages in creative, intuitive thought.

What gives the subconscious mind so much power is that it functions as the gateway to universal consciousness. Any thought, conviction, or intent present in your subconscious mind is communicated through universal consciousness. Remember, consciousness is a unified whole. Your subconscious mind is part of it. Just as any thought in your brain is communicated instantly across its neural networks, so, too, is any thought or feeling in your subconscious mind communicated across universal consciousness:

- Have you ever sensed that someone was watching you when there was no possible way you could see that person watching you, even in your peripheral vision? If so, you sensed the person because your subconscious mind perceived that person's subconscious energy.
- Have you ever felt a loved one's joy or suffering without being anywhere in the vicinity of that person where you could perceive physical signs of their joy or suffering? If so, you sensed the

person's psychic energy. It had an impact on your subconscious mind.

- Has a friend or relative ever mentioned something that you were thinking at that very moment? If so, you experienced a psychic connection. Your minds communicated at a subconscious level through universal consciousness.

We can often sense a person's psychic energy when they enter a room. We even have language to describe the phenomenon. We'll say something like, "Wow, you can really feel the temperature drop whenever Kyle enters the room." Or we describe someone as having a positive or negative vibe or a "hot" temper. The more mundane among us may explain the feelings we have around certain people as our emotional response to nonverbal communication from the other person, such as their posture and facial expression. While that's certainly part of how we communicate, it doesn't explain how we can sense a person's energy or know what they're thinking when we're not even in the same room with them.

We are connected to one another and to everything else in the universe through our subconscious minds. This connection is what gives the subconscious mind the power to draw the energy and resources we need and direct them in a way to manifest our subconscious desires in the physical world.

What Is the Mind?

The term *mind* is difficult to define. Many people think of the mind as whatever the brain does—record sensory perceptions, store and recall information, respond to stimuli, engage in logical thought processes, dream, imagine, coordinate body movement, monitor and control bodily functions, and so on. Dictionaries reflect this thinking. They define the mind as follows:

- Recollection, memory
- The element or complex of elements in an individual that feels, perceives, thinks, wills, and reasons
- Intention, desire

We often distinguish between body and mind. The body (including the brain) is physical. The mind isn't physical. You can think of the difference between body and mind as the difference between a digital device and its software; for example, between your smartphone (hardware) and its operating system, apps, and data (software). Your body and brain are physical (hardware), while your thoughts, feelings, and memories are mental (software).

However, in this book, we take a more expansive view of the mind: *Mind is the faculty for perceiving, recording, thinking, imagining, and directing.*

The mind is not a physical object. It cannot be perceived by any of the five senses—sight, hearing, taste, smell, or touch. Yet we know it exists. We perceive it through our self-consciousness, our self-awareness. It is not part of the body, but it is part of the individual—the part that is most characteristic of the individual.

In some systems of belief, the body is compared to a guest house with the mind being the guest living inside it. When the body dies, the mind remains intact—it retains some level of identity in universal consciousness. There is evidence for this belief. Some people have vivid recollections of past lives. However, this belief is controversial. We may never know for certain whether it is true.

What is true is that your mind is the key to your freedom. It is the source of your power to control your life. You may not be able to control what other people think or do (though you probably have some influence), but you have total control over your own thoughts and behaviors. You choose what to think and how to act.

Conscious versus Subconscious Mind

Your conscious mind is sometimes referred to as your objective mind because it deals with outward objects. The objective mind is aware of the objective world. Its means of observation are your five physical senses. Your objective mind is in charge of helping you navigate the physical environment. You gather input through your five senses, through observation, experience, and education.

If you visit the Grand Canyon, you experience it and learn about it through your five senses. You observe its incredible depth, fascinating rock formations, the rich colors of the different geological strata.

Your subconscious mind is often referred to as your subjective mind. It is aware of its environment, but not by means of the physical senses. Your subjective mind perceives by intuition. It is the control center of your emotions and the storehouse of all your memories. Your subjective mind performs its highest functions when your objective mind is suspended. It's the intelligence you experience when your conscious, objective mind is disengaged or in a sleepy, drowsy state.

Your subjective mind "sees" without eyes and "hears" without ears. It has the capacity of clairvoyance; that is, it can see and hear events that you can't physically observe. Your subjective mind can leave your body, travel to a distant location, and retrieve information just as if you had visited that place. Through your subjective mind, you can read the thoughts of others, read the contents of sealed envelopes, and know what's on a thumb drive without accessing its contents on a computer.

Your mind operates at two levels—conscious and subconscious. Neither is better or worse or weaker or stronger. The two work in tandem. Your conscious mind issues commands, and your subconscious mind, in concert with universal consciousness, carries them out.

CHAPTER 2

Unleash Your Mind Power

Pick up a flower on Earth and you move the farthest star.
—PAUL DIRAC, PHYSICIST

Have you ever solved a difficult problem in your sleep? You probably obsessed about it all day or all week or even for weeks on end. Then, one morning, you woke up knowing the solution. Where did that solution come from? Your conscious, rational mind was powerless to solve the problem, but your subconscious mind, knowing how important it was to you to find a solution, resolved the problem for you. And it did so effortlessly.

To get more in tune with the power of your subconscious mind, respond to the following prompts:

- Describe a time when you woke up knowing the solution to a difficult problem you had struggled with for a long time.
- Describe a time when you lost or misplaced something and knew where to find it as soon as you stopped consciously thinking about it.
- Have you ever thought about someone close to you and had them contact you out of the blue? Describe the incident.

- Do you and someone close to you seem to have a psychic connection? What has happened to make you think so?
- Have you ever had a sense that something bad was going to happen and it did? Describe the incident.
- Have you ever had a bad feeling about something that convinced you to avoid it, and you later found out that had you chosen differently, you would have suffered for it?
- Describe an activity or task that you can do without any conscious effort.
- Have you ever had someone enter your life unexpectedly who was perfectly suited to solve a difficult problem you were having or help you get something you really needed or wanted? Describe the experience.

Already, you have experienced the power of your subconscious mind without intentionally practicing any method for doing so and without fully understanding how your conscious and subconscious minds work together to mold your reality. In this chapter, you discover how your mind works and how you can begin to unleash its power.

How Your Mind Works

Your mind is your most precious possession. It is always with you, but its most amazing powers will be yours only when you've learned how to use it. As explained in chapter 1, your mind operates in two modes—the conscious (rational) and subconscious (creative). You think with your conscious mind, and whatever you think and accept as true sinks down into your subconscious mind, which then creates according to the nature of your thoughts. If you think good,

good will follow; if you think evil, evil will follow. This is the way your mind works.

The most important point to remember is this: As soon as your subconscious mind accepts an idea, it begins to execute it. Whether the thought is positive or negative, once accepted, the subconscious mind begins to make it happen. If your thinking is negative, your subconscious mind will ensure failure, frustration, and disappointment. When your thinking is harmonious and constructive, you will experience success, prosperity, and fulfillment.

Whatever you claim mentally and feel as true, your subconscious mind will accept and bring forth into your experience. All you need to do is get your subconscious mind to accept your idea. Once that happens, the law of your subconscious mind will bring forth the health, peace, and prosperity you desire. You give the command or decree, and your subconscious will faithfully reproduce the idea impressed upon it.

Planting Seeds of Thought

Have you ever heard the expression, "You reap what you sow?" Literally, it means you will harvest the crop you plant. If you plant apple seeds, you'll get apples. If you plant carrot seeds, you'll get carrots. Figuratively, it means that what you do now determines what your consequences will be later. If, for example, you don't study for a test, you're likely to do poorly on it. If you mistreat someone, you're likely to suffer the consequences later, either in the form of guilt or retribution (payback from the person you hurt).

This same analogy is useful for understanding how the conscious and subconscious minds work together. Imagine you're growing a garden in your mind. Your conscious mind is the gardener, your subconscious mind is the soil, and your thoughts and emotions are the seeds. Whatever you're thinking or feeling consciously are the seeds you're planting in your subconscious mind. Assuming that your thoughts and emotions reach the soil of your subconscious mind, they will grow and eventually produce a bountiful harvest—good or bad.

Thoughts of health, success, prosperity, and love will produce a harvest of the same. Likewise, thoughts of sickness, pain, poverty, hatred, failure, and disappointment will produce negative conditions and experiences. You can't plant weeds and expect to harvest grapes. Nor can you plant negative thoughts and emotions into the fertile soil of your subconscious mind and expect positive results in your life.

Begin now to sow thoughts of health, peace, happiness, right action, goodwill, and prosperity. Think quietly and with conviction on these qualities. Accept them fully in your conscious, reasoning mind. Continue to plant these wonderful seeds of thought in the garden of your mind, and you will reap a glorious harvest.

When your mind thinks correctly, when you focus on facts and challenge opinions, when the thoughts deposited in your subconscious mind are constructive, harmonious, and peaceful, the power of your subconscious will respond. It will bring about harmonious conditions, agreeable surroundings, and the best of everything.

Once you begin to control your thought processes, you can apply the powers of your subconscious to any problem or difficulty. You will be consciously cooperating with the infinite power and omnipotent law that govern all things.

Start now. Create two lists—one list of ten common negative thoughts and emotions you commonly have and a second list of ten positive, productive thoughts and emotions you would prefer to have. Then, put a conscious effort into focusing less on the negative items and more on the positive ones.

One Mind, Two Functions

You must remember that the conscious and subconscious are not two minds. They are two distinct functions of one mind. Your conscious mind is the reasoning mind. It is that phase of mind that chooses. For example, you choose your friends, the movies you watch, and the music you listen to. You make all your decisions with your conscious mind. On the other hand, without any conscious choice on your part, your heart beats, you breathe regularly, you digest the food you eat, and your body defends itself against infectious bacteria and viruses—all these complex functions are carried out by your subconscious mind independent of your conscious control.

Your subconscious mind accepts what is impressed upon it or what you consciously believe. It doesn't filter incoming data, analyze, reason things out, or make judgments as to what's good or bad as your conscious mind does. It responds according to the nature of your thoughts, emotions, and mental imagery. For example, if you consciously assume that something is true, even though it may be false, your subconscious mind will accept it as true and proceed to bring about results that must necessarily follow because you consciously assumed it to be true.

Hypochondriacs, for example, are highly susceptible to any mention of illness. If they hear that a cold is going around, they will almost certainly catch it. If they read about a rare illness on the internet, they will begin to experience its symptoms. In contrast, a doctor who believes that she is in perfect health will treat hundreds of patients with infectious diseases over the course of a week without becoming ill.

Hypnosis Reveals the Subconscious Mind in Action

Psychologists and others have performed countless experiments on people to illustrate the difference between the conscious, analytical mind and the subconscious, highly impressionable mind. How people respond to hypnosis clearly shows that the subconscious mind accepts suggestions without questioning them or challenging them. The subconscious mind will accept any suggestion, however false, and respond accordingly.

Hypnosis suspends the function of your analytical, conscious mind so that it is unable to question what you're being told. The hypnotist is then free to plant any idea or emotion into your subconscious mind that he desires. With a mere suggestion, he can convince you that your back itches, your nose is bleeding, you're a marble statue, or you're freezing. And you'll respond to the suggestion totally oblivious to any reality that might contradict it.

Hypnosis is a powerful tool often used constructively in the following applications:

- Smoking cessation
- Weight management
- Performance enhancement (school, work, athletics)
- Pain relief
- Memory recall or enhancement
- Stress management
- Overcoming phobias (such as a fear of public speaking or social anxiety)

Some people can put themselves into a hypnotic state to gain access to the memories and information stored in their subconscious minds and make their subconscious mind more receptive to suggestions.

If you could hypnotize yourself, what would you try to change about yourself in your hypnotic state? Would you try to eliminate a bad habit? Recall memories from the past? Improve your grades? Overcome a fear you have?

Remember, your subconscious mind is impersonal, nonselective, and accepts as true whatever your conscious mind believes to be true. Hence the importance of selecting thoughts, ideas, and premises that heal, inspire, and fill you with joy.

Your Subconscious Does What It's Told

Your subconscious mind is all wise. It knows the answers to all questions and the solutions to all problems. However, it doesn't question or challenge anything it's told. It doesn't argue with you or talk back. It doesn't cheer you on. It doesn't say, "Stop being so down on yourself" or "You go, girl!"

When you tell yourself, "I can't do this," "I'm not smart enough," "I can't afford _____," "Life sucks," or "Nobody loves me," you're planting these negative thoughts into your subconscious mind, and it responds accordingly. As a result, you're undermining your own good. You're bringing lack, limitation, and disappointment into your life.

When you set up obstacles, impediments, and delays in your conscious mind, you're denying the infinite intelligence and wisdom of your subconscious mind. You're saying in effect that your subconscious mind can't solve your problem. This leads to mental and emotional congestion followed by failure and disappointment. To empower your subconscious mind to deliver all the good you desire and deserve, affirm boldly several times a day:

> My subconscious mind is my gateway to infinite intelligence, power, and resources. I plant the seeds of my desires in the fertile ground of my subconscious mind, which will produce an abundant harvest. I am full of happiness and joy for myself and everyone in my life.

To have your subconscious solve a problem for you, give it the right request and get its cooperation. Your subconscious functions on autopilot, but it relies on your thoughts and emotions to specify the destination and develop a flight plan. When you request a solution to a problem, your subconscious will deliver it, but you must be totally confident in its ability to do so. Any doubt or uncertainty will undermine its efforts by diluting your request. You will simply be spinning your wheels—your mind will be busy and anxious, while you make little to no progress.

Still the wheels of your mind. Relax. Let go. Quietly affirm:

> My subconscious knows the answer. It is solving the problem right now. I am grateful for the perfect solution.

Repeat this affirmation throughout the day, while envisioning the problem solved. Envision how much better your life will be when the problem is gone. Imagine how relieved you will be and what you'll be doing when you're no longer wasting energy and focus on the problem.

CHAPTER 3

Tell Your Subconscious Mind What to Do: Affirmation and Other Techniques

People say I have created things. I have never created anything. I get impressions from the Universe at large and work them out, but I am only a plate on a record or a receiving apparatus—what you will. Thoughts are really impressions that we get from outside.

—THOMAS EDISON, INVENTOR

The key to engaging the power of your subconscious mind is knowing how to plant seeds of positive thought and emotion into its fertile soil. You cannot simply want or wish for something and have it appear. Desire must be combined with a strong positive emotion, such as one of the following:

- Appreciation
- Certainty
- Confidence
- Enthusiasm
- Faith/belief

- Gratitude
- Joy
- Love
- Optimism
- Relief

Positive emotion is the energy that brings your desire to a level of vibration in your subconscious mind that resonates with universal consciousness. Think of it as the sunlight that shines on the seeds of thought you plant into the fertile soil of your subconscious mind.

Beware of any negative emotions, which have the opposite effect, such as these:

- Anger
- Anxiety, worry
- Bitterness
- Disappointment, despair
- Doubt, uncertainty
- Envy, jealousy
- Fear
- Hate, resentment

Negative emotions draw negative energy. If you fear scarcity, hunger, or poverty, for example, fear will increase the vibration of your subconscious for all those conditions and begin to make them your reality.

Focus more on nurturing positive emotions in your consciousness than in purging negative emotions. Positive emotions are like light in darkness—so long as your mind is filled with light, the darkness of negative emotions cannot exist. If your heart is filled with love, there is no room for fear or hate. If you are totally confident in a positive outcome, you will have no fear or anxiety about the possibility of a negative outcome.

Various techniques can be used to plant the seeds of desire and positive thought into the fertile soil of the subconscious. This chapter presents several of the most effective techniques.

Autosuggestion

The term *autosuggestion* means suggesting something definite and specific to oneself. With autosuggestion, you state with your conscious mind what you want your subconscious mind to believe.

Autosuggestion is especially effective for countering negative statements from others (heterosuggestion) and negative self-talk. Whenever you hear, or start to say to yourself, something negative or self-defeating, replace it with a positive autosuggestion. For example, if you see something you want and begin to think, "I can't afford that," you say something positive such as, "I am wealthy beyond belief" or "My subconscious is the key to everything I want," and you imagine having that thing.

When composing a positive autosuggestion, follow these guidelines:

- **Keep it short.** Try to limit your statement to just a few words. You'll be repeating the statement several times throughout the day, so write a statement that you can easily memorize and recite.

- **Stay positive.** Focus on the solution, not the problem or challenge. For example, instead of writing, "My acne is gone" write something like, "My skin is clear." Instead of writing, "I am no longer poor," write something like, "I have all the money I need to pursue my dreams." If you mention the acne or the poverty, you're giving energy and focus to those things. Focus solely on what you desire, not the negative condition you want to go away.

- **Remain in the present.** Write your statement in the present tense, not past or future. For example, instead of writing, "I will be more confident," write something like, "I'm brimming with confidence."

- **Be yourself.** Be casual in your wording, as if you're writing to a close friend (instead of to your parents or a teacher you're trying to impress).

- **Envision your new reality.** Link your statement to mental images of how your life will be and how you will feel when your desire is realized. How will your friends and family members react? What will you be doing differently? Your mental images will not be part of your statement, but they will be recalled whenever you recite your statement. They may, in fact, be more powerful than the statement itself.

Affirmation

An *affirmation* is a statement declaring the truth of something. Its effectiveness is determined largely by your understanding of the truth and meaning behind the words. For example, if I were to say, "3 plus 3 equals 6," you could affirm that was true based on the mathematical principle of addition. You can affirm that the body can mend a broken bone that's set properly, because the fact adheres to physiological principles that govern the human body.

Principles exist. Their opposites do not. There is a principle of health but none of illness, a principle of harmony but none of discord, a principle of wisdom but none of ignorance, a principle of wealth but none of poverty, a principle of light but none of darkness. Just as dark is the absence of light, illness is the absence of health, poverty is the absence of wealth, discord is the absence of harmony, ignorance is the absence of wisdom, evil is the absence of good.

Through affirmation, you acknowledge what exists. When you affirm health, prosperity, and wisdom, you acknowledge that those things already exist. All you need to do is claim them for yourself. To affirm is to state that something is so, and as you maintain this attitude of mind—that what you desire already exists—regardless of any evidence to the contrary, what you affirm becomes manifest in your physical world.

When composing affirmations, follow the same guidelines given in the previous section for composing positive autosuggestions. However, your affirmations may be a little longer and more detailed (try to limit each affirmation to fifty words, so it will be easy to memorize and recite). The more definite and specific the language of your affirmations, the more powerful they are. When you affirm health, prosperity, and happiness for yourself or someone else boldly, confidently, and habitually, you plant the seeds in the subconscious for a future harvest of all these positive qualities and conditions.

Repeating an affirmation with understanding and conviction leads the mind to that state of consciousness where it accepts as fact what you state as true. Keep on affirming the truths of life until your subconscious responds accordingly.

The Art and Science of Affirmation

The power of affirmation is based in both art and science. The art is the technique or process you engage in. The science consists of the principles that govern how the subconscious responds to conscious thoughts and directives.

The infinite intelligence of your subconscious mind always responds to your conscious thinking. Whatever you want and request with a pure heart is yours to receive. But you must ask with certainty that your subconscious mind can and will deliver it. You must first create a clear image in your mind before your subconscious begins to act toward bringing it about. Your subconscious must have a clear destination before it can map a route to it.

Affirmation establishes the destination and your commitment and determination to reach that destination. When you practice affirmation, you are creating the reality you desire in your mind. That creation exists within your mind. Only then can your subconscious mind begin to attract the materials, energy, and other resources required to bring the idea to fruition in the physical world.

Make your affirmation in a state of happiness and peacefulness, looking forward to the certain accomplishment or manifestation of your desire. The sound basis for the art and science of affirmation is your knowledge and complete confidence that your subconscious mind always responds to your conscious thoughts and directives, and that your subconscious is at one with infinite power and intelligence. By stating your affirmation with complete confidence that your subconscious mind has the power to deliver what you want, you ensure that what you affirm will become manifest in your physical world.

The ability to bring forth what it is you desire is supported by people of all different religions and all walks of life. The Muslim boxer Muhammad Ali once said, "It's the repetition of affirmations that leads to belief. And once that belief becomes a deep conviction, things begin to happen."

Problem Solving

Your subconscious mind can guide you in making difficult decisions and solving challenging problems. Fully engage your conscious mind first, then pass the decision or problem to your subconscious mind to solve. Be totally confident that your subconscious will deliver the right decision or solution. Be free of doubt, fear, or worry.

Here are the steps of a simple technique you can use to receive guidance on any subject:

1. Quiet the mind and still the body. Tell your body to relax; it must obey you. It has no power to choose or make decisions.

2. Mobilize your attention; focus your thought on the solution to your problem.

3. During the day, analyze the issue or try to solve the problem with your conscious mind.

4. At the end of the day, as you lie in bed, hand over the decision or problem to your subconscious mind. Imagine how happy you'll be when the issue is resolved or the problem is solved. Let your mind play with this mood of happiness and contentment in a relaxed way as you doze off to sleep.

5. When you wake up, get busy with something else. The answer or solution is most likely to come when your attention is directed elsewhere. If it doesn't come to you by midday, repeat the steps.

In receiving guidance from the subconscious mind, the simple way is best. For example, suppose you lost or misplaced your house keys. You think about where you remember last having them, and they're not there. You search everywhere you think they could possibly be, and you can't find them. You recruit your friends and family members to help but to no avail.

Now is the time to get your best friend and all-knowing guide to help you. Talk to your subconscious mind the same way you'd talk to a friend. As you lie in bed at the end of the day say, "Hey, you know everything. You know where my keys are. Tell me." Then, as you fall asleep, imagine having your keys and the joy you'll feel when you find them. When you wake up, you'll have the answer.

You can't know the form the answer will take—it may be a mental image of where the keys are, the name of the person who knows where they are, the realization of where you last had them, or something else entirely. Just trust your intuition to guide you.

Self-Hypnosis

As explained in chapter 2, hypnotists can suspend the activity of the conscious mind to plant suggestions into a subject's subconscious mind. With practice, you, too, may be able to plant suggestions into your subconscious mind through self-hypnosis. To practice this technique, take the following steps:

1. Decide on what you want or want to change more than anything else right now. In other words, start with a strong desire.

2. Get comfortable in a quiet place where you'll be free from disruption for at least fifteen minutes.

3. Close your eyes and breathe slowly and deeply. Inhale through your nose and exhale through your mouth.

4. Imagine the infinite intelligence and power of universal consciousness flowing through you—flowing in through the top of your head and out through your feet.

5. Count down very slowly from 10 to 1, saying after each number, "I am going deeper and deeper." Continue to imagine cosmic consciousness flowing through you.

6. Recite your affirmation (from the earlier section on affirmation) twenty-one times, slowly and with meaning. (Studies have shown that when you repeat something twenty-one times, you begin to replace an old habit or a habitual thought.) Continue to imagine cosmic consciousness flowing through you.

7. Imagine, with all your senses, your world when the change has taken place or you've received what you wanted. Imagine how you will feel. Continue to imagine universal consciousness flowing through you.

8. Repeat three times, "I am, I do, and I have all I desire, and I am filled with gratitude and joy."

9. Open your eyes with a smile on your face.

Repeat these steps three times daily for at least one week.

Passing Over

Passing over involves using your conscious mind to persuade your subconscious mind to accept a request. It works best when used in tandem with self-hypnosis or when you're in a dreamlike state—for example, when you're falling asleep. To practice the passing over technique, take the following steps:

1. Know that your deeper mind is at one with infinite intelligence and power.

2. Calmly imagine what you want; see it coming into reality from this moment forward.

3. Let no thoughts of doubt or criticism enter your mind. Enter a mindful state of acceptance—the state of mind you had when you were a child, and you simply accepted ideas without questioning them.

4. Repeat your affirmation from the earlier section on affirmation. Relax and give over to the complete truth of your affirmation. Be like the little girl who had a very bad cough and a sore throat. She declared firmly and repeatedly, "It is passing away now. It is passing away now." Her illness passed away in about an hour.

The passing over technique is like the process of building a home. You start with a blueprint. You select only the best materials—the best wood, glass, and bricks, the best of everything. You make sure the builder follows the blueprint and best practices.

As you practice the passing over technique, think about the mental blueprint you have for your health, happiness, and self-fulfillment. What resources do you need to build the reality you desire? What knowledge, experience, and expertise will you require from yourself or others? Who can help you achieve your goals? What will they need to contribute? All your experiences and everything that enters into your life depend upon the nature of the mental building blocks that you use in the construction of your mental home.

You're continuously building your mental home. Your thoughts and mental imagery represent your blueprint. Hour by hour, moment by moment, you can build health, success, and happiness by the thoughts you think, the ideas you have, the beliefs you accept, and the scenes you rehearse in the hidden studio of your mind. Understand that you're constantly building the framework from which you experience everything around you—you're perpetually creating your personality, your identity, and your whole life story on this earth.

Build a beautiful mental home for yourself by realizing peace, harmony, joy, and goodwill right now. By dwelling on these things and owning them, your subconscious will accept your blueprint and bring all these things to pass.

Visualization

The easiest and most obvious way to formulate an idea is to visualize it, to see it in your mind's eye as vividly as if it were right in front of you. You can see with your eyes only what already exists in the external world; likewise, whatever you can visualize in your mind's eye already exists in the invisible realms of your mind. Any picture that you have in your imagination is as real as anything in the physical world. The only difference is that it exists in the nonphysical world of your mind. The idea and the thought are real and will one day appear in your physical world, assuming you don't waver from your mental image.

Visualization is the process of forming a mental image. These images then become manifest as facts and experiences in your life. Every house, apartment complex, office building, and skyscraper started as a visualization in the mind of an architect. It then became a drawing and maybe a plastic mold or a 3-D printout. The architect's mental image is projected into the physical world, where the structure is ultimately constructed.

The most accomplished athletes, performers, and public speakers practice visualization before a performance. They clear their minds of all distractions and imagine how they will perform, how they will feel, and how people in the audience will respond. They rehearse in their minds, so when the time comes to perform, they can do so with total confidence in the outcome. If they were to allow any worry or doubt to creep into their thoughts, it could shatter that confidence.

Suppose you've been asked to deliver a presentation to your local school board about your ideas for improving student performance from your perspective as a student and that of your fellow students. You've never been asked to speak in front of the school board. In fact, you're the first student at your school who has ever been invited to address the school board. You feel intimidated. "What if I forget what I'm talking about?" you ask yourself. "What if they ask me a question I can't answer?"

Of course, you'll want to prepare for the meeting by planning what you'll say, talking with your fellow students, and perhaps creating a PowerPoint presentation or preparing other materials to convey your ideas. But you also want to be confident and articulate, so you rehearse your presentation alone and maybe even in front of a few close friends and supportive family members.

As a confidence booster, you visualize the event ahead of time. You imagine the board members seated at a large table. They're eagerly anticipating your insights and ideas. As you begin your presentation, they're all very attentive, nodding in agreement with your brilliant insights and ideas. Likewise, the parents in attendance are watching your PowerPoint presentation and seem to be understanding and appreciating everything you're telling them. They're impressed that a student can deliver such a coherent presentation.

You maintain this visualization for ten minutes or longer, knowing and feeling that each audience member's mind and body are saturated with optimism, appreciation, and satisfaction. You allow your awareness to grow to the point at which, in your mind, you can almost hear the voices of the parents and board members speaking in support of you and your ideas.

Do this several times in the days before the presentation, and again directly before the meeting. As you're being introduced, let your heart fill with gratitude over the presentation you developed and the support of the people gathered to listen to you. Think about how great you'll feel afterward when the board members and parents thank you and express their confidence in your proposals.

Dream Boards or Vision Boards

One very popular and effective way to envision a desired outcome is to build a dream board or vision board—a collage of images, pictures, words, and affirmations that represent what you want. To build and use a dream or vision board, take the following steps:

1. Choose a theme for your board. Build your theme around something you want to be, do, or have. Maybe you want to be healthy and fit, go on an exotic vacation, or be student president.

2. Obtain a poster board or bulletin board.

3. Gather images, words, inspiring quotations, and other items that fit with your board's theme, engage your senses, and stir your emotions. The goal here is to create a collage that enables you to fully experience the object of your desire in your mind.

4. Spend a few minutes several times a day looking at your dream board and imagining the reality reflected in the board.

Mental Movie

You've probably heard the phrase, "A picture is worth a thousand words." If that's the case, then a movie is worth a million words. In fact, when movies were first invented, they were referred to as "motion pictures," and they were silent. These motion pictures projected on the screen the mental creations of their producers, directors, writers, and actors.

One effective way to visualize what you want is to project your mental creation on the blank screen of your subconscious mind. YouTube is an excellent tool for engaging in this process for certain applications. For example, if you want to learn to snow ski or water-ski, you can watch videos on YouTube to begin to develop the proper form and technique in your mind. You can begin to conceptualize yourself skiing before you actually do it. This mental movie will smooth the transition as you develop the physical coordination required.

I once used the mental movie technique to realize a strong desire I had to operate in the Midwestern United States.

At one time I wanted to have a permanent location in the Midwest, where people could find me if they wanted my help. I didn't know how to begin looking for the right situation, but the desire didn't leave my mind. One evening, while in a hotel in Spokane, Washington, I relaxed completely on a couch, immobilized my attention, and in a quiet, passive manner, imagined that I was talking to a large audience, saying in effect, "I'm glad to be here."

I saw in my mind's eye the imaginary audience, and I felt the reality of it all. I played the role of the actor, dramatizing my mental movie, and felt satisfied that this picture was being conveyed to my subconscious mind, which would bring it to pass in its own way.

The next morning, on awakening, I felt a great sense of peace and satisfaction, and in a few days' time I received an offer to lead an organization in the Midwest, which I accepted, and I enjoyed it immensely for several years.

The mental movie technique can be used for any number of situations—suppose you have a midterm in Spanish coming up. You studied hard, so you know the material, but you tend to experience anxiety when the time comes to take a quiz or test. To improve your performance, imagine yourself sitting calmly as the test is passed out. The teacher says you may begin, and you understand each question well, and the right answers come to you easily. Imagine that all you've learned is at the forefront of your mind. You can access it and use it well on the test. Imagine getting your grade and seeing that you performed as well as you had imagined you would.

As part of your mental movie, be sure to picture your happiness and pride in your good score and picture yourself feeling thankful that you were able to do so well. Each element of your mental movie is important. Each element reinforces the pattern of positive imagery in your subconscious mind. The mental picture held in the mind, backed by your confidence in it, will come to pass.

The mental movie technique can also be very helpful for enhancing athletic performance. For example, in preparation for a track event, you imagine yourself participating in the event and achieving your goal, whether it is to finish a race in a certain time, throw the discus a certain number of meters, or break the school's record for the high jump. In your mind, you hear the crowd cheering when you win, and you imagine your teammates and coach congratulating you on your incredible performance.

Mantra

A *mantra* is a word or phrase repeated in a quiet, meditative state. Chanting a mantra quiets the conscious mind and focuses it on the meaning of the word or phrase while bringing the subconscious into closer resonance with the object of the mind's focus. A mantra can be a very effective way to impress ideas or mental images upon the subconscious mind.

A mantra is generally shorter than an affirmation. Instead of limiting yourself to fifty words, limit yourself to no more than a few as in the following examples:

- Success
- Joy
- Confidence
- Adventure
- I am invincible.
- Prosperity is mine.
- I speak with confidence.
- I define my destiny.

A mantra can also be a sound you express that makes you feel good, such as "auhmmm" or "ohmmm" or simply humming to yourself. However, for the purpose of impressing thoughts or desires upon the subconscious, connect the mantra you choose to a clear mental image of what your life will be like when you have what you want. Try to engage all your five senses in this mental image along with how you will feel emotionally when your subconscious brings your desire to completion.

After you select a mantra, take the following steps to chant your mantra several times daily:

1. Sit or lie down in a comfortable, quiet place where you will be free of distractions and interruptions for at least fifteen minutes.

2. Close your eyes and focus on your breathing. Breathe slowly and deeply.

3. Repeat your mantra aloud for the duration of your meditation while imagining the infinite power and intelligence of universal consciousness flowing through you—flowing in through the top of your head and out through your feet.

4. As you repeat your mantra, focus on the mental image you associated with it. Imagine your life when this mental image becomes your reality. Imagine how amazing you will feel.

For example, suppose you feel as though your parents don't understand you or are too strict, or one of your parents frequently says or does things that hurt your feelings. To resolve the tension between you and your parents, envision the relationship you would like to have with your parents and associate that image with a mantra that you repeat several times throughout the day, such as "peace," "love," "harmony," or a calming sound like "ohmmm" or humming.

Before you fall asleep each night, lie in your bed, calm your mind, and let your body relax fully. Imagine you and your parents interacting in total harmony and happiness as you repeat your mantra. Think of peace, love, and happiness filling your parents as you doze off to sleep.

Remember that you and your parents and everyone in the world share one subconscious mind. Your thoughts of peace, love, and harmony will pass from your conscious thoughts to your subconscious mind and reach your parents, filling them with thoughts and feelings of peace, love, harmony, and joy. This is especially true if you go about your day feeling and demonstrating your positive thoughts and feelings in everything you do and in all your interactions with others.

The Sleeping Technique

A quiet, relaxed mind is more receptive to suggestion, and your mind is rarely quieter and more relaxed as it is just before you fall asleep. At this point, the conscious mind dozes off as the subconscious mind gears up for the night shift. In this state, the negative, limiting thoughts that tend to undermine your desire and conviction are themselves neutralized.

Suppose you want to get rid of a bad habit. As you lie awake in bed, instead of counting sheep, repeat over and over again, "I am [the opposite of the habit]." For example, if you have a habit of procrastinating, and not getting your schoolwork done on time, or even not getting out of bed quickly in the morning, you might repeat: "I am punctual and committed to excellence." If you tend to eat too many snacks and sweets, you might repeat, "I eat healthy, whole foods."

Repeat the phrase slowly, quietly, and with compassion for yourself for five to ten minutes at night and in the morning while lying in bed and still in a drowsy state. Each time you repeat the words, imagine yourself being exactly what you claim to be. When the urge comes to repeat the negative habit, repeat the phrase to yourself (and if no one's around, say it out loud). By doing so, you persuade your subconscious to accept the idea as true, and your bad habit disappears.

The "Thank-You" Approach

Universal consciousness loves gratitude and responds powerfully to it. The thankful heart is always close to the creative forces of the universe—in other words, when we're feeling and emitting gratitude, we're putting the creative power of universal consciousness to work for us. Gratitude attracts all that's good and pure.

Using gratitude to engage your subconscious mind is one of the easiest techniques. All you do is thank universal consciousness for delivering what you want while imagining having received it. It is also one of the most powerful techniques. Gratitude encourages you to envision what you're grateful for, it combines your desire with a powerful emotion, and it brings what you envision and how you feel about it into the present.

Logan was in a difficult financial situation. His bills were piling up. He was out of work, and he was worried about how to take care of his three children. Regularly, every night and morning, for a period of about three weeks, he expressed his gratitude using the words, "Thank you," in a relaxed, peaceful manner while imagining himself prosperous. He imagined having a fulfilling job with good pay, all his bills paid, and sitting at the dinner table with his wife and children sharing wonderful meals together.

He would repeat the phrase, "Thank you," until he was filled with gratitude. He imagined he was addressing the source of infinite power and intelligence within him, knowing, of course, that he could not see that power or intelligence. He was seeing with the inner eye of spiritual perception, realizing that his mental image of prosperity was the foundation for his prosperity.

By repeating "Thank you" over and over again, his mind and heart were lifted up to the point of acceptance. Whenever fear or thoughts of scarcity, poverty, or frustration entered his mind, he would say "Thank you" as often as necessary. He knew that as he maintained a deep and heartfelt gratitude, he would recondition his mind to the idea of prosperity, which is what transpired in his life.

A few weeks after he began expressing thanks, he ran into a former employer whom he had not seen for several years. The man offered him a well-paying job and advanced him some money to get by before his first paycheck was due. Now, the previously unemployed man has a senior position with the company, he is able to pay his bills, and he and his family are living a life of abundance. That simple two-word phrase transformed his mind, which then transformed his life.

As with any of these techniques, gratitude is a remarkably adaptive method for attaining your desire. And, yes, feeling gratitude for the car or iPhone you want—feeling gratitude for the thing as though you possess it right now—is an effective method for materializing that car or iPhone, but your subconscious mind can attract much more than material things.

Do you want to feel healthy and energetic? Do you want to feel confident and comfortable when you're with your classmates or colleagues? Do you want to have an active and happy social life? Start systematically and sincerely telling cosmic consciousness just how grateful you are to have these things, and how much you're enjoying them.

Feel the Love

Philosophers, poets, and religious leaders past and present have all heralded love as a powerful and transformative force: "Love conquers all." Love is a powerful creative force, as well, bringing two or more beings together to produce something that neither could produce on their own. It also brings your subconscious mind in perfect harmony with universal consciousness. When your heart is filled with love, no room remains for fear, frustration, or disappointment.

Filling your heart with love for everything that is true, good, and pure benefits you, but it can also be used to help your friends, family members, and loved ones through challenging times or to overcome sickness or grief. For example, suppose a friend contracts a viral infection and is being treated in the hospital. You would think of your friend's name and then quietly and silently fill your heart with the love you feel for your friend. Then, think of all the positive qualities of universal consciousness: love, joy, infinite intelligence, absolute peace, health, perfection, and beauty. Channel all the positive thoughts and emotions into universal consciousness, which permeates all beings, including your friend.

As you quietly think along these lines, your mind deeply connects with the universal consciousness, and you're lifted to a higher spiritual wavelength. You feel the infinite ocean of love dissolving everything unlike itself—anything imperfect, distorted, and unhealthy—in the mind and body of your friend. You feel all the power and love of universal consciousness laser focused on your friend, eradicating the virus and purging it from her body. The infinite ocean of life and love is flushing the virus from the body.

Issuing a Directive

Leaders in large organizations rarely invest time and effort into daily operations. They set the vision for the organization, establish goals, and issue directives to upper management. Upper management develops the strategy for executing the vision and meeting the goals. Then, they delegate the work through production managers, who delegate down to personnel. You, with your conscious mind, are the leader of your organization. Your subconscious is your upper management team. You develop a vision and set goals. Then, using your conscious mind, you issue a directive to your subconscious mind, which develops and executes the strategy for carrying out the directive.

Remember, your role is to develop a clear vision of the desired outcome and communicate it to your subconscious mind with conviction and confidence that your desired outcome will be achieved. Don't try to micromanage the process. A good leader assumes that the people she's in charge of know how to carry out their missions. When you realize that the power that created the universe is at your command, your confidence and assurance grow. You don't need to try to add additional power to your directive through great effort— just issue your directive with conviction.

For example, a young woman named Jackie wasn't interested in a romantic relationship with one of her classmates, Josh, but he wouldn't stop phoning and texting her and pressuring her for dates. He would wait outside the workplace by her car, and she found it very difficult to persuade him that she didn't want to pursue a relationship with him. She decreed as follows: "I release Josh into universal consciousness. He is in his true place at all times. I am free, and he is free. Through the power of universal consciousness, it is so." Jackie said afterward it was though Josh simply vanished from her life. He moved on, and she was no longer bothered by him.

You have the power to create your own reality simply by willing it into being. Remember, though, willing is not wishing. Wishing is a passive expression of desire. Willing is active intent.

Acting As If

William James, often regarded as the father of American psychology, stressed that the subconscious mind will bring to pass any firmly held mental image. He famously said, "Act as if what you do makes a difference. It does."

Over the years, the phrase "act as if" has been appropriated by both the New Thought and New Age movements to mean that if you act as though you've already gotten what you want or achieved your desired goal, the universe will bring it to fruition. You will be what you want to be. You will do what you dream of doing. You will have what you have the boldness to claim as yours.

You can think of "act as if" as one step beyond envisioning the desired outcome or playing a mental movie. Instead of merely holding the thought in your mind, you perform like an actor in a movie or play.

Here are a few ways to "act as if":

- If your desire is to be wealthy, be generous with the money and possessions you have, as if you're already wealthy.
- If you're looking for your soulmate, act as you'll feel when you've found that person. Presumably, you will be full of love, excitement, and joy, all of which are highly attractive qualities.
- Change your outer appearance, including the way you dress to clearly reflect the person you want to be or the position you want to have.

- Associate with people working in the profession you want to pursue. You may also want to shadow someone in the profession, have the person mentor you, or serve as their intern.
- If possible, alter your environment to reflect the environment that will exist when your desire comes about.
- Change your lifestyle to reflect your new reality. You may adopt new habits, engage in certain hobbies or pastimes, or hang out with different people.
- Test-drive the car you want to own.
- Visit the place where you dream of living.
- Attend a few classes at the college or university of your choice.

Acting as if crystallizes your mental image and generates the positive emotional energy required to impress that image onto your subconscious mind.

The Argumentative Method

The argumentative method stems from the work of Phineas Parkhurst Quimby, a pioneer in mental and spiritual healing, who lived and practiced in Belfast, Maine, over a century and a half ago. He was the father of psychosomatic medicine and the first psychoanalyst. He also had a remarkable capacity to diagnose clairvoyantly the cause of the patient's trouble, pains, and aches. Dr. Quimby used the method to convince his patients that their sickness was due to false beliefs, groundless fears, and negative patterns lodged in their subconscious mind.

With the argumentative method, you engage your mind in debate over what it has accepted to be true. For example, if you've convinced yourself that you're not smart enough to master a foreign language, force your mind to prove it. You may challenge the evidence. You may ask yourself whether you truly exerted enough effort in the past to learn another language. You may remind yourself that people who move to foreign countries and need to learn another language to survive almost always are able to learn that language. Are they truly smarter than you? You may even scold your subconscious for accepting the silly lie that you've told yourself.

Don't be afraid to talk back to your subconscious and refute any false notions that it tries to convince you are true. Remember, you're in charge. You give the orders, through your conscious mind, and your subconscious mind must obey.

Prayer

Prayer, when done properly, is affirmation. But prayer is often done improperly and, hence, fails to produce the desired results. People often make the mistake of praying for a cure to an illness or a solution to a problem. They're experiencing difficulty and seeking help to have that difficulty removed from their lives. In the process, their mind is focused on the problem instead of on the solution, and it is energized with a negative emotion, such as fear, worry, or doubt. As a result, their prayer is doing more harm than good. It is pouring more psychic energy into the problem or difficulty instead of into the solution.

The only difference between prayer and affirmation is that prayer is usually addressed to a Supreme Being based on the religious belief of the person composing or reciting the prayer. When composing a prayer, follow the same guidelines presented earlier in this chapter for composing an affirmation—keep it short, stay positive, remain in the present, and be yourself. When you recite the prayer, do so with complete confidence that your prayer is being answered, and envision how your life will be different and better as a result of your answered prayer. If you're praying for someone else, envision how their life will be different and better as a result of your answered prayer.

Also beware of any prayer you recite that you haven't written yourself. Review it carefully to be sure it follows the guidelines provided in the previous section. Don't recite a prayer that affirms a problem, an illness, or any other difficulty or causes you to feel a negative emotion. Reciting such a prayer will only lead to frustration and disappointment. Also, whenever you recite a prayer, do so with meaning—don't just say the words.

CHAPTER 4

Mind Power in Action— Real-Life Stories

Everyone who is seriously involved in the pursuit of science becomes convinced that a spirit is manifest in the laws of the universe—a spirit vastly superior to that of man, and one in the face of which we with our modest powers must seem humble.
—ALBERT EINSTEIN, PHYSICIST

As I lectured, preached, and wrote about the power of your subconscious mind over the course of my career, I would teach my techniques for engaging the subconscious mind to anyone who was willing and eager to listen. In the process, I gathered thousands of stories that demonstrate the power of the subconscious mind in real people's lives. This chapter presents a small selection of those stories.

A Dream Come True
A young boy, aged twelve, living in the United States, told his mother that he was going to visit his uncle in Australia during

school vacation. His thought of going was very strong, but he had another thought which said, "Mom won't let me go."

His mother had said, "It's impossible. We don't have the money, and your father can't possibly afford it. You're dreaming."

The boy explained to his mother that he had heard that if you desired to do something and believed that the creative intelligence within you would bring it to pass, it would happen.

His mother said, "Go ahead and believe what you like."

This boy, who had been reading extensively about Australia and New Zealand, had an uncle in Australia who owned a ranch. Daily and as the boy lay in bed at night, he repeated the following affirmation: "The creative spirit opens up the way for Dad, Mom, and me to go to Australia during vacation. I believe this, and the creative spirit takes over now." When the thought that his parents didn't have the money to go came to his mind, he would affirm, "The creative spirit opens up the way." His thoughts came in pairs, so he gave attention to the constructive thought, and the negative thought faded away.

One night, he had a dream in which he found himself on his uncle's ranch in New South Wales, viewing thousands of sheep and meeting his uncle and cousins. When he awakened the next morning, he described the entire scene to his mother, much to her amazement. The same day a letter came from his uncle inviting the three of them to his ranch and offering to pay their expenses both ways. They accepted.

The Shoulder Bag

On Christmas Eve, a young woman named Nina, a student at the University of Southern California, strolled through an exclusive shopping area in Beverly Hills. Her mind was filled with anticipation. She was about to spend the holidays with her family in Buffalo, New York.

As Nina passed a shop window, a beautiful Spanish-leather shoulder bag caught her eye. She looked at it yearningly. Then she noticed the price tag and gasped. She was about to say to herself, "I could never afford such an expensive bag," but she remembered something she had learned about the power of the subconscious mind: Never finish a negative statement. Reverse it immediately and wonders will happen in your life.

Staring through the glass, she said, "That bag is mine. It's for sale. I accept it mentally, and my subconscious sees to it that I receive it."

Later that day, Nina met her fiancé for a sendoff dinner. He arrived with an elegantly wrapped gift under his arm. Holding her breath, she unwrapped it. There was the identical leather shoulder bag she had seen that morning!

Nina had engaged the power of her subconscious mind to obtain the shoulder bag she wanted. She fully expected to receive it, and she turned the matter over to her subconscious mind, which has the power to accomplish anything.

Overcoming Stage Fright

Janet was a talented young singer. She was invited to audition for a leading role in a musical. She desperately wanted to audition, but she was terribly apprehensive.

Three times before, when she had sung for directors, she had failed miserably. The reason was fear of failure. She had a wonderful voice, but she had been telling herself, "When the time comes for me to sing, I'll sound awful. I'll never get the role. They won't like me. They'll wonder how I have the nerve even to try out. I'll go, but I know it'll be a failure."

Her subconscious mind accepted these negative suggestions as commands. It proceeded to manifest them and bring them into her experience. Her fear had transferred highly emotionalized counter-productive thoughts that in turn became her reality.

This young singer was able to overcome the force of her negative autosuggestions. She accomplished this by countering them with positive autosuggestion. What she did was this: Three times a day, she went alone into a quiet room. She sat down comfortably in an armchair, relaxed her body, and closed her eyes. She stilled her mind and body as best she could. She then repeated to herself, "I sing beautifully. I am poised, serene, confident, and calm." Three times during the day and as she lay in bed at night, she repeated this statement slowly, quietly, and with feeling five to ten times.

Within a week, she was completely poised and confident. When the fateful day came, she gave a wonderful audition and was cast in the leading role.

Becoming a Doctor

A young man in Australia grew up with a dream to become a physician. He was taking science classes and doing brilliantly, but he had no way to pay for medical school. His parents had both passed away. To support himself, he cleaned doctors' offices in the local hospital's professional building. He read that a seed planted in the soil attracts to itself everything it needs for its proper unfolding. All he had to do was to take a lesson from the seed and plant his vision of success in his subconscious mind.

Every night, as this young man went to sleep, he visualized a medical diploma with his name in big, bold letters. He found it easy to create a sharp, detailed image of the diploma. Part of his job was to dust and polish the framed diplomas hanging on the walls of the doctors' offices, and he studied them as he cleaned them.

He persisted with this visualization technique every night for about four months. Then one of the doctors whose office he cleaned asked if he would like to become a physician's assistant. The doctor paid for him to attend a training program where he learned a wide variety of medical skills, then gave him a job as his assistant. The doctor was so impressed with the young man's brilliance and determination that he later helped him through medical school. Today, this young man is a prominent doctor in Montreal, Canada.

This young man's success came because he had learned the law of attraction. He discovered how to use his subconscious mind the right way. This involved making use of an age-old law that says, "Having clearly seen the end, you have willed the means to the realization of it." The end in this case was to become a physician. He was able to imagine, see, and feel the reality of being a doctor. He lived with the idea. He sustained it, nourished it, and loved it.

At last, through his visualization, the idea penetrated the layers of his subconscious mind. It became a conviction. That conviction then attracted to him everything that was needed for the fulfillment of his dream.

Overcoming a Nasty Temper

Dan's problem was his constant irritability and bad temper. He was concerned about this himself, but if anyone tried to discuss it with him, he exploded in anger. He constantly told himself that everyone was picking on him and that he had to defend himself against them.

To counter this negative self-talk, he used positive autosuggestion. Several times a day—morning, noon, and at night prior to sleep—he repeated to himself:

> From now on, I shall grow more good-humored. Joy, happiness, and cheerfulness are now becoming my normal states of mind. Every day I am becoming more and more lovable and understanding. I will be a center of cheer and goodwill to all those around me, infecting them with my good spirits. This happy, joyous, and cheerful mood is now becoming my normal, natural state of mind. I am grateful.

After a month, his wife and his coworkers remarked on how much easier he was to get along with.

Restored Vision

A young man had severe eye trouble. His eye doctor told him he would have to have a delicate, risky operation. After learning about the power of the subconscious mind, the young man said to himself, "My subconscious made my eyes, and it can heal me."

Each night, as he went to sleep, he entered into a drowsy, meditative state. His attention was immobilized and focused on the eye doctor. He imagined the doctor was standing in front of him, and he plainly heard, or imagined he heard, the doctor saying to him, "A miracle has happened!" He heard this over and over again every night for five minutes or so before going to sleep.

Three weeks later he had another appointment with the eye doctor who had examined his eyes. The physician examined him again, then exclaimed, "This is a miracle!"

What had happened? This man impressed his subconscious mind, using the eye doctor as an instrument or means of convincing it and conveying the idea. Through repetition, certitude, and expectancy, he planted a mental image of recovery into his subconscious mind. His subconscious mind had made his eye. It held within it the perfect pattern or blueprint of the eye's normal, healthy structure. Once the subconscious was impregnated with the idea of restoring the eye to its healthy state, it immediately proceeded to heal the eye.

The Pharmacist

A young pharmacist named Mary worked in the prescription department of a big chain drugstore. One day while she was filling a prescription for me, we started talking. I asked her how she liked her work.

"Oh, it's fine," she said. "Between my salary and commissions, I do okay, and the company has a good profit-sharing program. With any luck, I'll be able to retire while I'm still young enough to enjoy life."

I was silent for a moment. Then I asked, "Was that the way you thought it would be as a child, when you decided you wanted to be a pharmacist?"

Her face grew troubled. "Well, no," she replied. "I guess not. I always saw myself with my own store. I wanted to walk down the street and have people say hello to me and call me by name. And I'd know all their names, because I was their pharmacist. You're going to think this is strange, but I even dreamed about having parents call me in the middle of the night because their kid was sick. I'd pull my clothes on over my pajamas and go down to the store to get them the medicine they needed. Not much like a nine-to-five job behind a counter at the back end of a big store, is it?"

"It certainly isn't," I said. "But why shouldn't you follow your dream? Wouldn't you be happier and more productive? Raise your sights. Get out of this place. Start your own store."

"How can I?" she said, shaking her head. "That takes big money, and we're just getting by from month to month."

My response was to share with her a wonderful fact: whatever she could conceive as true, she could bring into being. I went on to tell her something about the powers of her subconscious mind. She soon understood that if she could succeed in impregnating her subconscious mind with a clear and specific idea, those powers would somehow bring it to pass.

She began to imagine that she was in her own store. She mentally arranged the bottles, dispensed prescriptions, and imagined waiting on customers who were also her neighbors and friends. She also visualized a big bank balance. Mentally she worked in that imaginary store. Like a good actor, she lived the role. *Act as though I am, and I will be.* She put herself wholeheartedly into the act, living, moving, and acting on the assumption that she owned the store.

Several years later, Mary wrote me to say what had happened to her life since our conversation. The chain store she worked for went out of business because of competition from a larger store at a new mall. She found a job as a traveling representative for a major pharmaceutical company, handling a territory that covered several states.

One day her work took her to a small town on the western edge of her territory. There was only one drugstore in town. She had never been there before, but the moment she walked in, she recognized it. It was exactly the store she had visualized so clearly in her imagination.

Flabbergasted, she told the elderly owner of the drugstore about this amazing coincidence. In turn, the owner confided that he was about ready to retire but did not want to sell a store that had been in his family for three generations to some big corporation.

After several discussions, the owner offered to lend her the money to buy the store. She would be able to make the payments on the loan out of the profits of the business. The young woman moved her family to the town and soon was able to make a down payment on a big old house within walking distance of the store. Now, when she walks to work in the morning, everyone she passes says hello and calls her by name. They know her because she is their pharmacist.

Nikola Tesla

Nikola Tesla was a brilliant inventor. The Tesla coil is a crowd favorite. It's a transformer that produces high-voltage, low-current, high-frequency alternating-current electricity that can be transmitted through the airwaves like radio or TV signals instead of through electric cables. You can find plenty of YouTube videos demonstrating Tesla coils producing lightning bolts of electricity.

Tesla routinely engaged the power of his subconscious mind. Whenever he had an idea for a new invention or a new research direction, he would build it up in his imagination and then turn it over to his subconscious mind. He knew that his subconscious mind would work out the details and reveal to his conscious mind the knowledge he needed to build it. Through quietly contemplating every possible improvement, he wasted no time correcting defects. He would then pass this product of his creative, subconscious mind over to his technicians, who were given the task to build the proto-type.

In an interview, he said, "Invariably, my device works as I imagined it should. In twenty years there has not been a single exception."

He Fired Himself

Rafael was an executive in a major foundation. He admitted to me that for three years he had been terrified he would lose his position. He was always imagining failure. He kept expecting his subordinates to be promoted over his head. The thing he feared did not exist, except as a morbid anxious thought in his own mind. His vivid imagination dramatized the loss of his job until he became increasingly nervous and inefficient. Finally, he was asked to resign.

In reality, Rafael dismissed himself. His constant negative mental imagery, the flood of fear he sent to his subconscious mind, caused the subconscious mind to respond and react accordingly. It led him to make mistakes and foolish decisions. These in turn led to his failure.

Fear of Failure Conquered

An engineer said to me once, "I have failed to accomplish three assignments given to me. I failed miserably." This man began to see that he feared failure, and that he expected failure, so he decided to change his attitude. He admitted, "I have had faith in failure. From this moment forward, my faith will be in success." His motto became, "Anything I can conceive and believe possible,

I can achieve." He recited this daily, several times over the course of each day.

Yes, anything you can conceive, you can achieve. This engineer began to realize there was an infinite power within him, which he could tap. He began to find the answers, the power, and the wisdom to overcome challenges, which he previously believed to be hopeless. Now that he had faith in success, he expected success.

Confidence and certainty are as contagious as fear. As he replaced his fear with confidence, his subordinates grew in confidence, as well, and together they achieved ever increasing levels of success.

All She Wanted Was a Sewing Machine

Mary visited me after listening to one of my lectures in the Park Central Hotel in New York City. She asked the age-old question: "How can I learn to believe in myself?"

We are dealing with all levels of consciousness, and I met the girl at her level. I responded with a simple question: "What do you need most at this moment?"

I was expecting her to say something like "I want divine knowledge, truth, wisdom, and understanding." These, of course, are the highest desires, but her answer was, "A sewing machine!"

I explained that a machine is a creation of greater consciousness, of which her subconscious was an integral part. If she could form the idea of possessing the sewing machine in her mind, that thought would be made manifest in her physical world.

This is what she did: She sat down on her sofa one evening, became quiet, relaxed, stilled her mind, and imagined a sewing machine in front of her. She felt the reality and solidity of the machine with her imaginary hands, and she imagined using it. She went to sleep thanking the source of all things seen and unseen.

Days later, a woman who lived in the same apartment building knocked on Mary's door and asked her if she could use a sewing machine; she was leaving for her honeymoon and not returning, so she needed to get rid of it. Mary accepted!

CHAPTER 5

Repair the Damage: Overcome Self-Limiting Thoughts Implanted in Your Mind

All matter originates and exists only by virtue of a force which brings the particles of the atom to vibration. I must assume behind this force the existence of a conscious and intelligent mind. This mind is the matrix of all matter.

— MAX PLANCK, PHYSICIST

Many of us are raised on a steady diet of negative, self-destructive thoughts when we are at our most vulnerable—as children. Young minds are very receptive to suggestion. If a parent or teacher convinces us that we lack the intelligence or talent to be successful at a certain endeavor, it can lead to a life of scarcity and limitation. But only if we allow it.

The suggestions of others have no power over us unless we let them. Before a suggestion can impact our lives, it must be accepted by the subconscious mind, at which point that destructive thought in the mind of the other person becomes the destructive thought in our own mind. As soon as the subconscious accepts the thought, it begins to work toward bringing it into our experience.

In many ways, we are programmed as children to believe, speak, and behave as we do when we become adults. Our confidence or lack of it is also programmed into us during our years of early development. Fortunately, we have the power to reprogram ourselves by changing our thoughts and emotions. We have the power to redirect our thoughts and emotions from a negative path to a positive one. And as we transform how we think and feel, we begin to experience a positive transformation in our lives.

Heterosuggestion

A *heterosuggestion* is an idea that one person presents to another person intending the other person to accept it. In all ages and in every part of the world, the power of suggestion has played a dominant role in the development of individuals and the communities in which they live. Customs, religions, political movements, and entire societies develop and flourish as populations adopt shared attitudes and beliefs. These are then reinforced and passed on from one generation to the next through heterosuggestion.

Heterosuggestion can be used as a tool to rally people around a common cause, energize a community, and reinforce positive values. However, it can also be misused to command and control others. When used constructively, it can help to build harmonious, productive, and free societies. When used destructively, that same power can fuel hatred, division, and injustice. Its results can be enduring patterns of failure, misery, sickness, and disaster.

Negative Self-Talk

Negative heterosuggestion is only one source of harmful thoughts and emotions. It's the external source. There is also an internal source. Many of us engage in negative autosuggestion or self-talk. We have a habit of "beating ourselves up" or, more accurately, "beating ourselves down."

We tell ourselves that we're not good at math or English, that we're not athletic or musically inclined or artistically talented. We convince ourselves that the whole world is against us and we will never succeed at anything. We may even start to think that we're unlovable. As a result, we go through life frustrated, disappointed, and discouraged—victims of our own self-fulfilling prophecy.

Negative self-talk can lead to serious issues that undermine happiness and success, including the following:

- **Self-limitation:** You need at least a tiny bit of confidence to try to do anything outside your comfort zone. Negative self-talk can sap your confidence and convince you that trying isn't worth the effort.

- **Catastrophizing:** Catastrophizing is a form of distorted thinking in which you perceive even a minor setback as a total failure. It often convinces people to give up when they're very close to success.

- **Depression:** Chronic negative thinking impacts mood, leading to depression, which can impair performance in all areas of a person's life.

- **Insecurity:** Negative thinking is often related to insecurities, which can undermine a person's ability to form and maintain productive, rewarding relationships. Insecurities can even lead to blaming and criticizing others for one's own perceived short-comings.

Take Inventory

From the day we are born, many of us are bombarded with negative suggestions from authority figures in our lives—parents, teachers, coaches, community leaders, newscasters, and others we trust to teach us and tell us what is true. In our youth, we rarely question what we're being told, so we tend to accept what we're told. Unfortunately, much of what some of us have been taught and have accepted as true are negative, self-limiting beliefs.

How many of the following self-limiting beliefs you have come to accept and possibly repeat to yourself regularly?

- I'm just lazy.
- I'm always late.
- I never stick with anything. (I never finish what I start.)
- I can never do anything right.
- What's wrong with me?
- I don't deserve something so good.
- I'm too old (or too young).
- I'm not smart enough.
- I just don't have the money.
- Nobody cares what I say.
- People are selfish.
- The world isn't fair.
- Other people are holding me back from what I want to achieve.
- What is meant to happen will happen. (I have no control over what happens.)

- I'm not good with money.
- Everything is too expensive.
- I can't afford to be happy.
- I'll never find the right partner.
- Relationships only cause pain.

Carry a pen and a pad of paper with you, and over the course of the next few days, jot down the negative, self-limiting thoughts that enter your mind (they may be statements you make to yourself or statements you hear others say to you).

By accepting negative, self-limiting suggestions, you collaborate in bringing them to pass. As a young child, you may have been helpless. You didn't know any better. Now, as a teenager or young adult, you don't have any excuses. You are entirely in control of what you choose to think. You can recondition your mind, with constructive autosuggestion, to think more constructively and counteract the negative impressions from the past.

The first step is to make yourself aware of the suggestions that are operating on you. These can be statements you picked up from others (heterosuggestions) or those you've composed and repeat to yourself (autosuggestions). Unexamined, these mental impressions can create behavior patterns that cause failure in your personal and social life. Constructive autosuggestion can release you from the mass of negative verbal conditioning that might otherwise distort your life pattern and make the development of good habits difficult or even impossible.

Pay close attention to the thoughts, emotions, and mental images that enter your brain throughout the day. You don't need to be at the mercy of destructive suggestions. Most of us have been exposed to negative, limiting beliefs at all stages of our lives. If you look back, you can easily recall how parents, friends, relatives, teachers, and associates held you back with their negative suggestions.

Study what was said to you, closely examine their underlying meanings, and you will discover that many of the negative, self-limiting statements you were being told were nothing more than a form of propaganda. Their concealed purpose was—and is—to control you by instilling fear in you.

This propaganda goes on in every home, school, office, worksite, and club. You will find that many of the suggestions people make, whether they know it or not, are aimed at making you think, feel, and act as they want you to, in ways that are to their advantage, even if they're destructive to you.

Reprogram Your Mind

Read the news online or watch it on TV. Every day, dozens of stories sow the seeds of fear, anxiety, and disappointment. If you let them in and accept them, these thoughts can cause you to lose your zest for life. However, once you understand that you don't need to accept these thoughts, they have less influence over what you think and how you feel. In fact, you have the power to ignore them completely. You can turn off your TV, avoid news-based websites, and even choose not to log into your social media accounts.

As for the negative, self-limiting thoughts that have been planted in your mind already, you can begin to challenge them, argue against them, and counter them with opposing thoughts and emotions, such as the following:

- Life is amazing!
- I am energized and enthusiastic.
- I'm always punctual.
- I persist in the face of adversity.
- I am perfect in all ways.
- I deserve all the good that life has to offer.
- A person is never too young or old to pursue their dreams.
- Through the power of my subconscious mind, I have access to infinite intelligence.
- I live in a universe of abundance. Wealth is mine to claim.
- People listen and care about what I say.
- Most people are generous and caring.
- The power of the subconscious mind is available to everyone.
- Nobody can stand in my way unless I let them.
- I choose. I command. My subconscious mind obeys.
- I accept only perfect health and fitness.
- Happiness is a state of mind. I choose to be happy.
- The right people are attracted to me.
- All my relationships are rewarding and harmonious.
- My soulmate is in the world and is being drawn to me.

Flip back to the list of negative, self-defeating thoughts you created earlier in this chapter and write a new list of empowering thoughts to counter them.

Whenever a discouraging thought starts to enter your mind, interrupt it, replace it with its contradictory empowering thought, and repeat the empowering statement several times slowly and with conviction. The goal here is to ultimately replace your discouraging self-talk with its positive counterpart.

The Power of an Assumed Major Premise

Since the days of ancient Greece, philosophers and thinkers have studied the form of reasoning called a *syllogism* (pronounced *SILL-oh-jizm*). Your mind reasons in syllogisms. In practical terms, this means that the premises your conscious mind accepts as true determine the conclusion your subconscious mind will come to, no matter what the question or problem might be. If your premises are true, the conclusion must be true.

For example:

Every virtue is praiseworthy;
Kindness is a virtue;
Therefore, kindness is praiseworthy.

Or this:

Everything made by people changes and passes away;
The pyramids of Egypt are made by people;
Therefore, the pyramids will change and pass away.

The first statement in each of these three-line syllogisms is referred to as the major premise, the second is the minor premise, and the final statement is the conclusion.

A college professor who attended some of my science-of-mind lectures in New York City's Town Hall came to speak with me afterward. He told me, "Everything in my life is topsy-turvy. I have lost health, wealth, and friends. Everything I touch turns out wrong."

I explained to him that his problems followed logically and directly from his self-destructive major premise. To change his life, he needed to establish a new major premise in his thinking. He needed to accept as true the conviction that the infinite intelligence of his subconscious mind was guiding, directing, and prospering him spiritually, mentally, and materially. Once he did that, his subconscious mind would automatically direct him wisely in his decisions, heal his body, and restore his mind to peace and tranquility.

This professor formulated a mental image of the way he wanted his life to be. This was his major premise:

Infinite intelligence leads and guides me in all my ways. Perfect health is mine, and the law of harmony operates in my mind and body. Beauty, love, peace, and abundance are mine. The principles of right action and divine order govern my entire life. I know my major premise is based on the eternal truths of life, and I know, feel, and believe that my subconscious mind responds according to the nature of my conscious mind's thinking.

Later he wrote me the following progress report: "I repeated the statements of my major premise slowly, quietly, and lovingly several times a day. I knew that they were sinking deep down into my subconscious mind. I was convinced by the laws of mind that results must follow. I am deeply grateful for the advice you gave me, and I would like to add that all aspects of my life are changing for the better. Your system works!"

CHAPTER 6
Get Healthy and Fit

The power that made the body heals the body.
—B. J. PALMER, DOCTOR OF CHIROPRACTIC

The human body is amazing. Perhaps more amazing is the brain's ability to keep it running twenty-four hours a day, seven days a week, 365 days a year . . . 366 days a year on leap years. Your body is fully equipped to defend itself against deadly viruses and even repair broken bones, cuts, strained muscles, and damaged tissues and organs. When doctors perform a liver transplant, the donor's liver grows back to normal size after the surgery, and the transplanted part grows into an entirely new liver in just a few weeks! Imagine having a car that could repair itself and grow new parts.

A growing body of evidence suggests that our thoughts and emotions play a bigger role in our health and well-being than most of us realize. The connections between the nervous, muscular, endocrine, respiratory, cardiovascular, digestive, immune, and excretory systems influence the onset and course of many illnesses. Unfortunately, conventional medicine focuses primarily on physical treatments—medications, surgery, radiation, and chemotherapy—and ignores, for the most part, psychological and emotional factors that disrupt proper function. As a result, patients are often treated as passive recipients of healthcare instead of as active participants in their own healing.

The truth is that, for a large part, we are responsible for our own health and well-being. Certainly, some factors may be outside our control, such as a genetic defect or susceptibility, physical injury, or exposure to environmental toxins or infectious bacteria or viruses. But we strongly influence our physical health through our conscious choices of where and how we live, what we put in our bodies, and how we think and feel.

Give Your Body What It Needs

To maintain or restore optimal health and fitness, you must supply your body with the following essentials:

- **Proper nutrition:** The right amounts and ratios of macronutrients (protein, fat, and carbohydrates) and micronutrients (vitamins, minerals) are necessary to provide the body with the energy and chemical building blocks it needs for growth and repair.
- **Clean air:** Like most animals, humans need oxygen to survive, which, fortunately, is present in the air we breathe. Ideally, that air should be free of toxins, irritants (such as dust), and pathogens (harmful bacteria, viruses, and fungi).
- **Pure water:** The human body is about 60 percent water (and the brain is about 85 percent). The body uses water as a solvent, transport medium, lubricant, and coolant. As a solvent and transport medium, it plays an essential role in flushing toxins from the body. Like air, the water we drink should be free of toxins, impurities, and pathogens.

- **Physical and mental activity:** Physical and mental activity are essential for the development of strong minds and bodies. Physical exercise builds strength, endurance, and coordination, while mental exercise increases blood flow and oxygen delivery to the brain to support neuron growth and development and build new neural networks.
- **Restorative sleep:** Although everyone is different, most people need about eight hours of quality sleep per night for daily repair and restoration. During sleep, your body detoxes, replenishes energy reserves, repairs damaged cells and tissues, and processes the data collected over the course of the day.
- **A positive mindset:** By positive mindset I mean low stress. Stress increases muscle tension and restricts blood flow, which can lead to poor digestion, headaches, muscle tension and pain, high blood pressure, heart disease, stroke, poor sleep, weight gain, cognitive impairment, and other chronic health issues.

To support your body's ability to function optimally, follow these suggestions:

- Eat healthy whole foods (not processed), mostly plants—vegetables, fruits, and nuts.
- Get plenty of fresh air. Spend time outside, preferably in nature. Air out your home as much as possible, assuming you don't live in a highly polluted area.
- Drink quality water, at least two quarts daily (you can find daily recommended water intake charts on the internet). Avoid sweet drinks like soda and even fruit juice and any drinks with additives, including energy drinks.
- Remain active physically, socially, and mentally. Walk, ride your bicycle, have fun with friends and family members, play sports

and games, find a hobby. Don't sit around watching TV, surfing the web, or hanging out on social media all day.

- Get at least eight hours of sleep per night. Don't pull all-nighters. Lack of sleep traumatizes the brain more than you might think.
- Identify the source of any stress you feel, and then fix it or forget it. Resolve issues or let them go.
- Don't poison your body with alcohol, marijuana, nicotine, caffeine, junk food, and other harmful substances.

Remember, many health issues originate in the mind in the form of thoughts or emotions, but even when the cause is mostly physical, the mind can play a key role in healing and recovery.

Focus on Health, Not Illness

If you tune into the mainstream media, you can't help but notice that we pay far more attention to illness than we do to health. We are inundated with advertisements for medications available to treat a wide variety of illnesses—allergies, asthma, diabetes, eczema, psoriasis, indigestion, high blood pressure, chronic pain, headaches, depression, anxiety, and more.

By implication, we are falsely led to believe that our bodies alone are incapable of perfect health. Worse, perhaps, is that these messages have the potential to plant the seeds of these diseases into our subconscious minds

During the early days of the COVID-19 pandemic, the 24/7 news coverage filled people with fear and anxiety over the novel coronavirus instead of confidence in the body's immune system to protect itself against infection. Stories focused on infection rates, hospitalizations, and deaths. How many stories did you hear about people who had COVID-19 and experienced no or only mild symptoms? How many reports did you hear or read providing advice on how to support or boost your body's immune system? Health authorities and the news media even downplayed and, in some cases, discounted the natural immunity people developed from a COVID infection.

To be healthy and fit, focus more on health and less on illness. Celebrate your good health and be grateful for it. Avoid news stories and advertisements that feed your mind information about illnesses. All those stories and ads serve as negative suggestions, planting the idea of illness in your subconscious mind.

Whenever thoughts of pain or illness enter your mind, counter them with thoughts of perfect health and well-being. For example, if you begin to feel as though you're coming down with a cold, remind yourself that you are perfectly healthy and that your immune system stands guard at all hours of the day and night to protect you against infection. Consider repeating the following affirmation:

I am in perfect health. All my body's systems function optimally and in perfect harmony to maintain my health and fitness. My immune system stands guard. It instantly identifies, attacks, and destroys all bacteria and viruses that pose a threat to my health.

Embrace health. Reject illness.

One Universal Healing Principle

Many alternative healthcare practices rely on the power of the subconscious mind to cure illness and restore health. These include faith healing, meditation, mindfulness, biofeedback, hypnosis, visualization, guided imagery, music/sound therapy, the emotional freedom technique (EFT), and the use of placebos—a harmless pill or procedure that has no therapeutic effect other than to convince the patient of its effectiveness. All these practices have documented cures for even the most severe and persistent illnesses, and they are all based on the following truths:

- Your mind has two faculties—conscious and subconscious thought.
- Suggestions can be planted through your conscious mind into the fertile soil of your subconscious mind.
- Your subconscious mind has complete control over your body's function.

The symptoms of almost any disease can be induced in a person through hypnotic suggestion. For example, a subject in the hypnotic state can develop a high temperature, flushed face, or chills according to the nature of the suggestion given. You can suggest to the person that he is paralyzed and cannot walk, and it will be so. You can hold a cup of cold water under the nose of the hypnotic subject and tell him, "This is full of pepper; smell it!" He will sneeze violently and repeatedly. What do you think caused him to sneeze? The water, or the suggestion?

If someone tells you he is allergic to Timothy grass, you can place a synthetic flower or an empty glass in front of his nose, when he is in a hypnotic state, and tell him it is Timothy grass. He will develop his usual allergic symptoms. This shows us that the cause of the symptoms is in the subconscious mind. Curing the symptoms also takes place in the subconscious mind.

Different schools of medicine, such as osteopathy, chiropractic, chi gong, acupuncture, and naturopathy, all produce remarkable healings. So do the rites and ceremonies of the various religious beliefs throughout the world. It is obvious that all these healings are brought about through the subconscious mind—the only healer there is.

Notice how the subconscious mind heals a cut on your finger. It knows exactly how to do it. The doctor dresses the wound and nature heals it. But nature is nothing more than another name for natural law—the law of the subconscious mind. The instinct of self-preservation is the first law of nature, and self-preservation is the foremost function of the subconscious mind. Your strongest instinct is the most potent of all autosuggestions.

Unload Your Emotional Baggage

John E. Sarno, MD, author of the *New York Times* best seller *Healing Back Pain: The Mind-Body Connection* contends that approximately 85 percent of back pain and 78 percent of headaches don't have an identifiable biological cause. Dr. Sarno has treated thousands of patients with back pain who show no signs of structural abnormalities via medical imaging (such as x-rays) that would account for their pain.

In a large majority of back pain patients, the pain is self-inflicted. It's triggered by emotional factors that increase muscle tension and reduce blood flow to certain areas of the body. Dr. Sarno refers to this medical condition as tension myositis syndrome (TMS). It is the physical manifestation of repressed emotion.

According to Dr. Sarno, TMS is a defense mechanism to protect against emotional pain. The physical pain distracts our minds from a deeper emotional pain that we may think we have no control over. Instead of dealing with difficult situations or emotions, people with TMS inflict physical pain on themselves—a pain that they subconsciously believe they have more control over. They then occupy their minds by seeking solutions to their physical pain through medications, surgery, physical therapy, and other interventions. Dr. Sarno notes that in many patients, when pain is relieved in one area of the body, it moves to other areas—for example, from the lower back to the neck or shoulders.

He believes that other physical ailments can serve the same purpose as TMS—to distract us from our emotional pain. He provides the following list of the most common ones:

- Acne
- Asthma
- Chronic constipation or diarrhea
- Dizziness
- Eczema
- Frequent urination
- Hay fever
- Headaches
- Hives
- Indigestion
- Psoriasis
- Ringing in the ears

If you're experiencing a chronic medical condition, and your doctor cannot identify a root cause, you may be dealing with a frustrating situation or emotional pain buried so deep you're unaware of it. Examine your life and your feelings closely by conducting the following emotional inventory. On a separate piece of paper, write down any emotions in the following list that apply to you:

- Anger/resentment
- Anxiety/worry

- Bitterness
- Disappointment
- Fear
- Frustration/powerlessness
- Guilt
- Loneliness
- Low self-esteem
- Sadness
- Shame

If you placed a checkmark next to any of the emotions in the list, you have some work to do. First, you need to find the source of the emotion, which could be a situation you're dealing with right now, something that happened in the past, or something you're concerned about that hasn't even happened yet. Then, you need to take action to release that emotion. You typically have three choices:

- Fix it (resolve the problem)
- End it (as in a toxic relationship)
- Let it go (make a conscious decision not to let it impact your life)

The specific action you need to take varies based on the emotion and its root cause. If you feel guilt, for example, you may need to apologize to the person you feel you harmed and pay some sort of restitution. If you're angry or bitter over a wrong you suffered in the past, you may need to forgive the guilty party. Holding onto anger is likely to harm you far more than the other person. In a way, all forgiveness is self-forgiveness in that it releases the burden of anger and bitterness. When you forgive someone, you're freeing yourself from having to carry around that negative emotional baggage.

How I Healed Myself

The most convincing evidence anyone can have of the healing power of the subconscious mind is a personal healing. In midlife I developed a malignant skin cancer. I went to the finest doctors who tried the most advanced treatments medical science could offer. None of these helped. The cancer became progressively worse.

Then, one day, a clergyman with a deep store of psychological knowledge explained to me that my subconscious mind had fashioned and molded my entire body from a tiny original cell. He said that since my subconscious mind had made my body, it could also re-create it and heal it according to the perfect pattern within it.

This clergyman pointed to his watch. "This had a maker," he told me. "But before the watch could become an objective reality, the watchmaker had to have the idea of it clearly in mind. If for some reason the watch stopped working as it should, the watchmaker's idea of it would give him the knowledge he needed to fix it."

I understood what he was trying to tell me by this analogy. The subconscious intelligence that created my body was like the watchmaker. It knew exactly how to heal, restore, and direct all the vital functions and processes of my body. But for it to do this properly, I had to give it the perfect idea of health. This would act as cause, and the effect would be a healing.

I formulated a very simple and direct affirmation:

My body and all its organs were created by the infinite intelligence in my subconscious mind. It knows how to heal me. Its wisdom fashioned all my organs, tissues, muscles, and bones. This infinite healing presence within me is now transforming

every cell of my being, making me whole and perfect. I give
thanks for the healing I know is taking place at this time. Wonderful are the works of the creative intelligence within me.

I repeated this simple affirmation aloud for about five minutes
two or three times a day. After some three months, my skin was
whole and perfect. The malignancy had vanished. My doctor was
baffled, but I knew what had happened. I had presented life-giving
patterns of wholeness, beauty, and perfection to my subconscious
mind. These forced out the negative images and patterns of thought
lodged in my subconscious mind, which were the cause of all my
trouble.

Nothing appears on your body except when the mental equivalent is first in your mind. As you change your mind by drenching it
with incessant affirmatives, you change your body.

This is the basis of all healing.

Thanks to universal consciousness the power to heal—the
infinite healing presence—is available to you. Simply feel that
power within yourself, create a message using it, and release your
message. Universal consciousness hears and accepts your message.
This may sound hard to believe, and I, too, struggled at first with
the idea. But having had my own healing experience, which I dis-
cussed with a doctor, it started to make sense. I know that universal
consciousness exists; my mind and body are manifestations of it.
Healing, as an abstract possibility, exists, and therefore I have the
power to access it with my subconscious mind. I can tap into it,
affirm it, and release it into the greater consciousness, where it is
affirmed again. The ancient proverb says, "The doctor dresses the
wound, and nature heals it."

Stories of Transformation

Joe Dispenza healed himself of spinal cord injuries after a serious bicycle accident that left him paralyzed. Instead of undergoing the radical spinal surgery that his doctors recommended, he decided to enlist the power of universal consciousness to repair his spine. He checked out of the hospital and spent six weeks reconstructing his spinal column, piece by piece, in his mind, following a mental blueprint he had formed there. He also envisioned the day he would be able to leave his wheelchair and walk again. Within ten weeks, he could feel the physical transformation in his body as movement gradually returned to his limbs.

Now, Dr. Dispenza treats patients by training them how to use the power of their subconscious minds to heal themselves. I strongly encourage you to visit his website at DrJoeDispenza.com and scroll down to the Stories of Transformation and watch at least two of the videos of patients who put his training into practice. Their stories are truly inspirational, and they reveal the incredible power of the subconscious mind in healing the body and restoring health and function. For more videos, go to YouTube.com and search for Dr. Dispenza.

Your Story

As you put what you learn in this book into practice, you will begin to experience the benefits for yourself. As you do, write your own story of how the power of your subconscious mind improved your life in some way. Did you use the power to cure an illness, get something you always wanted, achieve a goal, optimize your performance, establish fulfilling relationships? Document your experience and share it with others.

CHAPTER 7
Make Lots of Money

To attract money, you must focus on wealth. It is impossible to bring more money into your life when you are noticing you don't have enough, because that means you are thinking thoughts that you do not have enough.
— RHONDA BYRNE, AUTHOR OF *THE SECRET*

You have a fundamental right to be rich. You are here to lead an abundant life; to be happy, radiant, and free; to grow, expand, and unfold spiritually, mentally, and materially. You should, therefore, have all the money you need to lead a full, happy, and prosperous life and to surround yourself with beauty and luxury. Why be satisfied with just enough to go around when you can enjoy the abundant riches of your subconscious mind?

In this chapter, you will learn to make friends with money. Once you do, you will always have everything you need and more. Don't let anyone make you feel ashamed of your desire to be rich. At its deepest level, it is a desire for a fuller, happier, more abundant life. It is a cosmic urge.

Money Is a Mental Construct

Money is a symbol of exchange. It is a symbol not only of freedom from want, but of beauty, refinement, abundance, and luxury. It's also a symbol of the economic health of the nation. When your blood is circulating freely in your body, you're healthy. When money is circulating freely in your life, you're wealthy—economically healthy. When people begin to hoard money because they're greedy or they fear losing it, the cash flow slows or even stops, leaving them financially ill and morally bankrupt. After all, what good is money if it is not increasing health, happiness, and fulfillment and making the world a better place?

As a symbol, money has taken many forms throughout the centuries. Almost anything you can think of has served as money at some time and place in history—gold and silver, of course, but also salt, beads, and trinkets of various kinds. Now we use paper money, coins, checks, and digital currency. Regardless of the form it takes, money is constructed first in the mind and then made real in the physical world. It is a mental construct.

To become wealthy, first build the idea of wealth in your mind. Imagine yourself wealthy. What does that look like to you? Where are you living? What are you doing and with whom? How do you feel when you have everything you ever wanted and then some? How do your friends and family members respond to your financial success? Take some time to put your vision into words. Describe your imagined experience of being wealthy.

Think Rich, Be Rich

As soon as you understand the power of the subconscious mind, you have within your grasp the key to riches of all kinds—health, material possessions, great friends, talents, knowledge, wisdom, and more. Everyone who has taken the trouble to learn the laws of mind knows that they will never be poor in any sense of the word. Regardless of economic crises, stock-market fluctuations, recessions, strikes, rampant inflation, or even war, they will always be amply supplied.

They live a life of abundance because they have conveyed the idea of wealth to their subconscious minds. As a result, their subconscious keeps them supplied even when those around them are experiencing scarcity. They have convinced themselves in their minds that money is forever flowing freely in their lives and that there is always a surplus. As they decree it, so it is. If the economy collapses tomorrow and everything they possess becomes worthless, they will continue to attract wealth. They will come through the crisis comfortably and likely even benefit from it.

Why Most People Lack Money

As you read this chapter, you may be thinking, "I deserve more money than I have." In my opinion, that is true of most people. They really do deserve to have more—but they're unlikely to get it. One of the most important reasons these people do not have more money is that they silently or openly condemn it. They refer to money as "filthy lucre." They tell their children and friends that "money is the root of all evil." They may even believe the false notion that being poor is virtuous. It is not. You can do far more good if you are rich than if you are poor. It is usually the rich who build businesses that provide opportunities for the poor. It is usually the rich who build organizations to aid the poor. You are no better or worse because you have lots of money or lack it.

Take an inventory of your own thoughts and emotions about money. How many of the following statements do you believe are true?

- Money is the root of all evil.
- Money can't buy happiness.
- It's better to be poor and happy than rich and sad (as if those are the only two options).
- The rich get richer, and the poor get poorer.
- I hate money.
- Money is a curse.
- If you want to be rich, you must be born rich.
- Wealthy people are immoral or unethical.
- I won't do what it takes to be wealthy. (Implying that the only way to make money is to harm or take advantage of other people.)
- Rich people are greedy.

If you checked any of the boxes, the first order of business is to reverse your thinking about money. Here are some positive affirmations that can help (choose one or more affirmations and repeat them several times daily):

- Money is a means to opportunity and self-fulfillment.
- Money enables me to live a life of abundance.
- I can help more people if I am rich than if I am poor.
- Wealth is manufactured by the human mind.
- There is plenty of money for everyone. I don't have to take money from someone else to have it for myself.
- Money comes to me easily.
- I am a money magnet.
- Being wealthy feels amazing.
- I am grateful to be financially free.

Don't think about money in terms of accumulating it and being rich. Think of it in terms of what you can use it to accomplish, the experiences you can afford to have, the people you can help, the good you can do, and how you can use it to more fully develop and express yourself. Money is not a goal. It is not an end to seek. It is a means to an end. It's neither good nor evil except in how it's used.

Purge your mind of all negative beliefs about money. Never regard money as evil or filthy. You can't attract what you criticize. If you criticize money, it will flee from you.

Hard Work Is Not Required

If you're having financial difficulties and struggling to make ends meet, it means that you have not convinced your subconscious mind that you will always have plenty and some to spare. It's not a matter of working eighty hours a week. Yes, many people have worked hard all their lives to become wealthy, but some people make as much or more working only a few hours a week. Those who struggle are the people who have convinced themselves that financial success requires most of their time and energy.

Don't believe that the only way to become wealthy is through hard work. It is not so; the effortless way of life is the best. Do what you love to do, and it will feel effortless. Expect and accept the riches that come from doing what you love and doing it well. Trust your subconscious mind to deliver the wealth and abundance you deserve for your passionate pursuits.

I know an executive in Los Angeles who earns hundreds of thousands of dollars a year in his position. Last year he went on a nine-month cruise seeing the world and visiting some of the most beautiful places on the planet. He said to me that he had succeeded in convincing his subconscious mind that he is worth that much money. He told me that there are people in his organization earning about one-tenth as much as he does who know more about the business than he does and could probably manage it better. However, they have no ambition and no creative ideas. They don't leverage the power of their subconscious minds.

Don't Envy What Others Have

Envy is a negative emotion expressing a scarcity in one's own life. For example, if you're envious of a friend who has nicer clothes and the latest high-tech gadgets, takes more extravagant vacations, and has more fun than you, you're admitting a lack of all that in your own life. Your thinking is likely to drive everything you envy away from you and toward your friend.

Instead of envy, be happy for those living in abundance and be grateful for all you have. Don't compare yourself to others. There will always be people who have more money than you and those who have less, people in higher positions and those in lower ones, people who have more friends than you and those who have fewer, people who are more talented than you and those who are not nearly as talented. Engage your conscious and subconscious minds in more productive pursuits and nurture positive emotions of love, joy, and appreciation. Focus your mind on a fuller life for yourself.

Money and a Balanced Life

One time a man came up to me and said, "I am broke. But that's all right. I don't like money. It's the root of all evil." These statements represent the thinking of a confused, neurotic mind. Love of money to the exclusion of everything else will cause you to become lop-sided and unbalanced. You are here to fully enjoy life and achieve self-fulfillment, and you live in an environment of abundance. Rejecting money is like rejecting a life of abundance, enjoyment, and self-fulfillment. Nobody thinking clearly would reject all that goodness.

If you set your heart on money exclusively and say, "Money is all I want; I am going to give all my attention to amassing money; nothing else matters," you can get money and gain a fortune, but at what cost? You have forgotten your mission—to live a full life. Your pursuit of money is only a secondary objective for achieving your primary goal—self-fulfillment.

You would not need money if someone gave you everything you needed to fulfill your mission. In fact, some people lead full lives without money, or without much money, through a more direct exchange of goods and services. They may care for a property in exchange for food and a place to live. They may work on a yacht to satisfy their desire to travel around the world. They may work as an intern in exchange for an education. They may, like social media influencers, exchange their influence for valuable products and ser-vices. They may develop mutually beneficial relationships with rich friends who finance their dreams and desired lifestyles. The only difference when money is involved is that the money serves as a less direct means of exchange.

Whether you choose a direct or indirect means of exchange, maintain your focus on your overall mission—to live a full and ful-filling life.

People who make money their sole aim are usually sorely dis-appointed when they achieve their goal. They soon discover, after all their efforts, that money wasn't all they needed. No one on their deathbed wishes they had spent more time making money. They also need loving relationships, rewarding work, memorable experiences, and the joy of contributing to the success and welfare of others. Don't focus exclusively on money. Focus instead on what you'll do with that money and how it will improve your life and the lives of others.

By learning the laws of your subconscious mind, you can have a million dollars or many millions, if that's what you want, and still have everything else you need to live a full life and achieve a high level of self-fulfillment.

Developing the Right Attitude Toward Money

Here is a simple technique you may use to attract money. Repeat the following statements several times a day:

> I love money. With enough money, I can be, do, and have everything I want. Money enables me to achieve higher levels of self-fulfillment and to help others. I use it wisely and constructively. Money is constantly circulating in my life. I release it with joy, and it returns to me multiplied in a wonderful way. Money flows to me in avalanches of abundance. I am grateful to live such a rich and wonderful life.

How to Earn More Money at Work

Many people earn less at their place of employment because they have a negative attitude toward their work, their employer, their supervisor, or themselves. For example, suppose you have a part-time job, you feel that you're being underpaid, and you believe that your supervisor doesn't respect you or appreciate the work you do. These thoughts are likely to lead to feelings of bitterness and resentment. They'll negatively impact your productivity and your relationships, not only with your direct supervisor but also with your coworkers and perhaps even with customers or clients.

By setting yourself in mental opposition to your employer, you're subconsciously severing your ties with that business. You're setting a process in motion. Depending on the level of negative impact you have, the process could lead to your termination, which would likely deepen your feelings of bitterness and resentment. But how can you blame your supervisor or employer? Essentially, you fired yourself. Your supervisor was merely the instrument through which your own negative mental state was made manifest in your life.

To earn more, make yourself worth more to your employer or more attractive to other prospective employers by maintaining a positive attitude. Start by feeling good about yourself and the work you do. Then, extend your positive attitude to everyone you interact with at work—executives, managers, coworkers, customers, and vendors. Look for ways to improve the business and make those around you more successful.

As you increase your value to your employer, don't hesitate to demand the compensation you deserve. Never settle for less than you know you're worth. And if your current employer won't pay you what you deserve, pursue other options—other employers in the same business. Or start your own business. Or invent a new product or service.

What's most important is that you maintain a positive mindset and engage your subconscious mind to find your path to the wealth you desire and deserve. If you become angry or discouraged, you will only undermine your efforts to advance.

Protect Your Investments

If you're seeking guidance regarding investments, or if you're worried about your stocks or bonds, quietly claim the following:

> Infinite intelligence manages all my financial transactions. Whatever I invest in will prosper.

If you do this frequently, with certainty, you'll be guided to make wise investments. You'll also be protected from loss, because you'll be prompted to sell any risky securities or holdings before they lose value.

You Can't Get Something for Nothing

In large stores, cameras and security systems are in place to monitor shoppers and keep people from stealing. Nearly every day in some areas they catch people trying to get something for nothing. Anyone who does such a thing is steeped in a mental atmosphere of lack and limitation. In trying to steal from others, they are robbing themselves of peace, harmony, faith, honesty, integrity, goodwill, and confidence.

Criminals don't understand or appreciate the power of their subconscious minds. They lack confidence in the source of limitless supply. If only they would mentally call on the powers of their subconscious mind and claim that they are guided to their true expression, they would find honest work and abundance. Then, by living with honesty, integrity, and perseverance, they would become a credit to themselves and to society at large.

Being lazy is another form of theft. Don't expect to receive something for nothing. As you enrich your own life and develop your intelligence, talents, and skills, contribute to the world around you. Contribute doesn't just mean donating money, material goods, or your time. It can also involve anything you do that fulfills your own life or enriches the lives of others, such as installing and repairing heating and air conditioning systems; delivering an outstanding performance as a singer, dancer, actor, or athlete; learning to play a musical instrument; or inventing a time-saving device. Just don't sit around all day repeating the benefits of other people's accomplishments.

Your Constant Supply of Money

The path to freedom, comfort, and limitless supply lies in recognizing the powers of your subconscious mind and the creative power of your thought or mental image. Accept and expect abundance in your own mind. Your mental acceptance and expectation of wealth is the first step toward drawing it into your life. As you enter into the mood of opulence, all things necessary for the abundant life will come to pass. Let this be your daily affirmation; write it in your heart:

I am one with the infinite riches of my subconscious mind. It is my right to be rich, happy, and successful. Money flows to me freely, copiously, and endlessly. I am forever conscious of my true worth. I give of my talents freely, and I am wonderfully blessed financially. Life is awesome!

CHAPTER 8

Be Confident:
Overcome Shyness and Fear

Mind is a wave of the ocean of Being.
—Maharishi Mahesh Yogi, Spiritual Teacher

The biggest obstacle that most people encounter on their road to health, wealth, success, and self-fulfillment is lack of confidence. And nothing is so obviously a product of the mind than confidence. Confidence is a choice. You can choose to be afraid, timid, and apprehensive or confident, courageous, and bold. These are all emotions entirely within your control.

- Make a list of the ten most confident people you know.
- Make another list of the ten most successful people you know.
- Review your lists. Chances are good that the two lists contain many of the same names.

Confident people are successful people, and successful people tend to be the most confident. Confidence builds success, and success builds confidence. But to achieve success, you must have at least the confidence to try.

If you lack self-confidence, you're missing out on opportunities for success and opportunities to achieve self-fulfillment. You're settling for less in life than you deserve, and you are cheating the rest of us out of everything unique about you that you have to offer. This chapter will help you engage the power of your subconscious mind to begin to build confidence and overcome fear and shyness in your life.

Overcoming Fear of Speaking in Public

One of my students was invited to speak at the annual banquet of his professional association. He told me he was panic-stricken at the thought of speaking in front of a crowd of a thousand people, many of whom were influential in his field. He overcame his fear this way: For several nights he sat calmly in an armchair for about five minutes. He said to himself slowly, quietly, and with certainty:

> I am confident in my knowledge and expertise. I am prepared to deliver an outstanding presentation and answer even the most challenging questions. I speak with poise and confidence. I am relaxed and at ease.

By repeating this affirmation, he persuaded his subconscious mind to accept it. It became his reality in his mind where it was then ready to be made manifest in his physical reality. When his time came to speak, he overcame his fear and delivered a successful presentation.

The subconscious mind is amenable to suggestion. It is controlled by suggestion. When you still your mind and relax, the thoughts of your conscious mind sink into the subconscious. As these positive seeds of thought sink into the subconscious, they flourish and produce an abundant harvest.

Your Greatest Foe

In the midst of the Great Depression, during his inaugural address to the nation, US President Franklin Delano Roosevelt said, "Let me assert my firm belief that the only thing we have to fear is fear itself—nameless, unreasoning, unjustified terror which paralyzes needed efforts to convert retreat into advance."

It is true. The only thing we have to fear is fear itself. Fear is the root cause of failure, sickness, war, and lack of progress. Millions of people live in fear, and their fears are usually unfounded. They fear that which hasn't happened—potential failure, illness, old age, poverty, hunger, war, and death. As a result, they fail to make the most of the present and to fully enjoy their lives. Even worse, fear can lead to panic, and panic often results in irrational action that can worsen a situation.

Good Fear, Bad Fear

Fear is nothing more than a thought triggered by a real or imagined threat. For example, if you're walking along a path in the woods and suddenly notice a mountain lion walking down the same path toward you, you're likely to experience a sensation of fear that triggers a fight, flight, or freeze response. You basically have three choices—fight the mountain lion, run away from it, or stay perfectly still, hoping it won't attack you. This sense of fear is good, for the most part—it's part of your biological self-defense mechanism.

However, baseless fears can cause unnecessary mental anguish. For example, a small child can be paralyzed with fear when a sibling says there's a monster under the bed who will grab him in the night when he's asleep. But when the parent turns on the light and shows that there is no monster, the child is freed from fear. The fear in the mind of the child was every bit as real as if there were a monster under the bed, but the source of the fear was fictional. There was no monster to fight or flee from, no reason to freeze in fear. The effective response was to correct the small child's false belief by presenting the truth.

A newborn baby has only two basic fears, the fear of falling and the fear of sudden loud noises. These fears are normal. They serve as a sort of alarm system given you by nature as a means of self-preservation. Normal fear is good. You hear an automobile coming down the street toward you and you step aside to avoid getting hit. The momentary fear of being run over compels you to move out of the way to remain safe.

All other fears are abnormal, usually taught to us by well-meaning parents, relatives, teachers, and others who have irrational fears of their own.

Document Your Fears

Take the following steps to create an inventory of your fears so that you can start to develop a better understanding of them:

1. On a blank piece of paper, create a four-column table. Label the columns as follows:
   - Fear
   - Source
   - My response
   - Impact on my life

2. In the Fear column, name your biggest fears or the ones that are most disruptive and self-limiting. Here's a list to get you started thinking about what your fears may be:
   - Fear of failure
   - Fear of rejection
   - Fear of change
   - Stage fright or fear of public speaking
   - Fear of loneliness or abandonment
   - Social phobia
   - Fear of contracting a disease
   - Fear of angering or disappointing someone
   - Fear of dying
   - Fear of flying
   - Fear of commitment
   - Fear of pain

3. In the second column, describe the source of your fear—the person, place, thing, or event causing your fear. Note whether it is an actual threat or anticipated—something that you're worried will happen in the future.

4. In the third column, describe how you're responding to the threat or how you plan to respond. Think of your action in terms of fight, flight, or freeze. Are you confronting your fear, avoiding it, or unable to act because you're unsure what to do?

5. In the fourth column, describe how the fear and/or your response to the fear is impacting your life. Is it discouraging you from doing or pursuing something that might benefit you, something you might enjoy? If you've acted on the fear, has your action made the situation better or worse, and in what way?

Challenge Your Fear's Trigger

Fear can be tough to pin down. It often begins as fear and quickly turns to anger, which is like a futuristic cloaking device for fear. It makes you think you're angry about something when what's really going on is that you're afraid of something. In addition, a big source of fear is ignorance, especially when you're convinced that you know something when you really don't know the truth. So when you're afraid, it's easy to jump to conclusions, assume the worst, and overreact. It's important to fully understand what's going on, so you can make rational decisions.

For example, recently I ordered a soundbar for my flat-screen TV for $250 and received an email confirmation from the company. After two weeks, the soundbar still hadn't arrived. I visited the company's website and called the phone number listed on the site. I called about ten times over the course of several days and at different times each day, and the number was always busy. I clicked a link on the site to contact customer support via email and asked for an update about my order. My email was bounced back with an indication that the address I was using was wrong.

I started to get angry, but then I realized that the source of my anger was really fear. I feared losing my $250 and not receiving the product I had ordered. My fear led me to believe that I was being scammed, which made me angry. However, I had no way of knowing whether I was being scammed. Both my fear and my anger were the result of my ignorance—my not knowing what was really going on with my order and not knowing whether the company was legitimate.

My first impulse was to file a dispute with my credit card company and to report the company to the Federal Trade Commission,

but then I noticed that the email address I received my order confirmation from differed from the email address link I clicked on
the company's website. So I tried to contact the company again by
responding to the confirmation email I had received after placing
my order. I wrote the following:

> Please provide me with an update on order #: 14283737006
> 9090-1275. I have tried to call the phone number on your web-
> site, but it is always busy, and the email address on your About
> Us page is in error. Not being able to contact you makes me
> feel as though I am being scammed. Please let me know when
> you receive this and provide an update on my order to put my
> mind at ease.

Within twenty-four hours, I received the following response via
email:

> Thanks for letting me know about the phone and email issues.
> I checked with the warehouse today and they said production
> is running about three weeks on the soundbar you ordered.
> I apologize for the delay. Between the holiday shutdown and
> supply issues, production is taking longer than normal. Just
> let me know if you cannot wait and I can cancel the order and
> refund your charge.

I was glad that I didn't overreact and write an angry letter to
the company or take action to get the company in trouble with my
credit card company or the FTC. I would have felt bad had I done
that. Within three days of writing to the company, I received the
soundbar I had ordered, and it was just what I wanted.

One big source of fear, and anger, is ignorance. Whenever you feel fear or anger, ask yourself, "What do I think I know?" and then ask yourself, "Is what I think I know true or am I just assuming the worst?" If you don't really know what you think you know, it's time to do some digging to find out the truth. Often, fear can be alleviated simply by asking the right people the right questions and clearing up any misunderstanding.

Do What You Fear

Nineteenth-century philosopher and poet Ralph Waldo Emerson, once wrote, "Do the thing you are afraid to do, and the death of fear is certain." Emerson's advice is the foundation for psychotherapies such as exposure therapy and immersion therapy. There's even a version of exposure therapy that employs the use of virtual reality. With exposure therapy, a person is gradually exposed to whatever they fear until they feel comfortable around it. For example, if someone suffers from arachnophobia (fear of spiders), they might start by looking at photos of spiders, then watching videos, and gradually working their way up to holding a tarantula.

There was a time when I was filled with unutterable fear at the thought of standing before an audience and speaking. If I had given way to this fear, terrible as it was, I am sure you would not now be reading this book. I would never have been able to share with others what I have learned about the workings of the subconscious mind.

The way I overcame this fear was to follow Emerson's advice. Quaking inside, I stepped in front of audiences and spoke. Gradually I became less fearful, until at last I was comfortable enough to enjoy what I was doing. I even grew to look forward to speaking engagements. I did the thing I was afraid to do and slayed my fear.

When you affirm positively that you're going to master your fears, and you come to a definite decision in your conscious mind, you release the power of your subconscious mind, which flows in response to the nature of your thought.

Fear of Failure

I often get visits from students who attend a university near me. One complaint many of them share is what we can call "suggestive amnesia" during examinations. They all tell me the same thing: "I know the material before the exam, and I remember all the answers after the exam. But when I'm in the classroom staring down at a blank exam booklet, my mind goes totally blank!"

Many of us have had similar experiences. The explanation lies in one of the major laws of the subconscious mind, which is this: the idea that realizes itself is the one we pay the most attention to. In talking with these students, I find that they're most attentive to the idea of failure; they're afraid of failing. As a result, it's failure that the subconscious mind brings into reality. The fear of failure itself creates the experience of failure by way of a temporary amnesia.

A medical student named Sheila was one of the most brilliant students in her class. Yet when she faced a written or oral examination, she found herself going blank at even simple questions. I explained the reason to her. She had been worrying about failing for several days before the exam. These negative thoughts became charged with fear.

Thoughts enveloped in the powerful emotion of fear are realized in the subconscious mind. In other words, this young student was telling her subconscious mind to see to it that she failed, and that is exactly what it did. On the day of the examination, she was struck by suggestive amnesia.

As Sheila learned about how her subconscious mind works, she came to realize that it's a massive data storage facility. It contains a perfect record of everything she had heard and read during her medical training. Moreover, she learned that her subconscious mind responds to suggestions and requests most effectively when mind and body are in a relaxed, peaceful, and confident state.

Every night and morning, she imagined her parents congratulating her on her wonderful academic record. She would hold an imaginary letter from them in her hand. As she began to contemplate this happy outcome, positive emotions of pride and joy welled up inside her.

As Sheila continued to stimulate her mind with positive thoughts and emotions, the all-wise and omnipotent power of her subconscious mind took over. It dictated and directed her conscious mind accordingly. She imagined the end, thereby willing the means to the realization of that end. After following this procedure, she had no trouble passing her subsequent exams. The subjective wisdom of her subconscious mind took over and compelled her outstanding performance.

Fear of Water

When I was about ten years old, I accidentally fell into a swimming pool. I had never learned to swim. I flailed my arms, but it did no good. I felt myself sinking. I can still remember the terror as the water surrounded me. I tried to gasp for air, but my mouth filled with water. At the last moment, another boy noticed my plight. He jumped in and pulled me out. This experience sank into my subconscious mind. The result was that for years I feared the water.

Then one day I mentioned this irrational fear of mine to a wise elderly psychologist.

"Go down to the swimming pool," he told me. "Look at the water. It is simply a chemical compound, made up of two atoms of hydrogen and one of oxygen. It has no will, no awareness. But you have both."

I nodded, wondering where this was leading.

"Once you understand that the water is essentially passive," he continued, "say out loud in a strong voice, 'I am going to master you. By the powers of mind, I will dominate you.' Then go into the water. Take swimming lessons. Use your inner powers to overcome the water."

I did as I was told. Once I assumed a new attitude of mind, the omnipotent power of the subconscious responded, giving me strength, faith, and confidence. It enabled me to overcome my fear, and I mastered the water. Today I swim every morning for both health and pleasure.

Don't hand over power to inanimate objects. Don't allow them to master you. You are the one with the mind, so you have the power to conquer any physical challenge. You simply need to put your mind to it.

Using Your Imagination to Overcome Fear

Your imagination is a powerful tool for overcoming fear because it enables you to confront your fear in your mind first, without exposing your body to any physical threat. It also helps you build confidence. As you succeed in overcoming your fear in your mind, you increase your confidence in overcoming your fear in the physical world.

Suppose you're afraid of swimming. Sit still for five or ten minutes three or four times a day. Put yourself into a state of deep relaxation. Now imagine you're swimming. Subjectively, you *are* swimming. Mentally you have projected yourself into the water. You feel the brisk coolness of the water and the movement of your arms and legs. It is all real and vivid—a joyous activity of the mind.

You're not just daydreaming. What you're experiencing in your imagination will be developed in your subconscious mind. Over time, you'll feel compelled to express physically what you imagined mentally as such a pleasurable experience. The next time you try to swim, you'll do it with joy instead of fear.

You can apply the same technique to overcome other fears. If you're afraid of high places, imagine taking a stroll in the mountains. Feel the reality of it all. Enjoy the pure air, the alpine flowers, the thrilling scenery. Know that as you continue to do this mentally, you will come to do it physically with ease and comfort.

Overcoming the Fear of Riding in an Elevator

Jonathan was an executive with a large corporation. For many years he was terrified to ride in an elevator. He would walk up seven flights of stairs to his office every morning to avoid the elevator ride. When he had to meet with people from other companies whose offices were on higher floors, he always found some excuse to meet them at his own office or at a restaurant. Business trips out of town were torture for him. He had to call ahead, to make sure his hotel room was on a low floor and that he would be able to use the stairs.

This fear was the product of his subconscious mind, perhaps in response to some experience that he had long since forgotten on a conscious level. Once he learned this, he set about to change it. He began to praise the elevator every night and several times a day. In a calm, confident mood, he repeated this to himself:

> The elevator in our building is a wonderful idea. It is a product of the universal mind. I ride in it in peace and joy. In my imagination I am now in the elevator. It is full of our employees. I talk to them, and they are friendly, joyous, and free.
>
> I remain silent now while the currents of life, love, and understanding flow through the patterns of my thought. I step out of the elevator and head toward my office.

He continued repeating this affirmation several times daily for ten days. On the eleventh day, he walked into the elevator with other members of his company and felt completely free.

Catastrophizing

Catastrophizing is a form of distorted thinking that assumes conditions are worse than they are or that an outcome will be far worse than it's likely to be.

I knew a woman who was invited to go on a trip around the world by plane. She was afraid of flying, and she fed her fears by researching airplane crashes. She even ordered a video of the world's worst airplane crashes and spent hours watching it. She imagined herself going down in the ocean and drowning. That's catastrophizing. Had she continued engaging in this distorted thinking, she would likely have experienced what she feared most. Fortunately, she chose to adopt more positive thought patterns and had a wonderful time.

A businessman in New York was less fortunate. He had been very successful and prosperous until a tiny seed of worry found its

way into the fertile soil of his subconscious mind. Over time, he created his own private mental motion picture in which his company
was forced into bankruptcy, and he lost everything. The more he
played this movie of failure in his mind, the more he sank into a
deep depression. He refused to stop this morbid imagery. He kept
telling his wife, "This can't last," "The boom will end any day now,"
"It's all hopeless, we're going to go broke."

His wife later told me that in the end he did go bankrupt. All
the things he had imagined and feared came to pass. The things
he feared did not exist, but he brought them to pass by constantly
fearing, believing, and expecting financial disaster.

The world is full of people who are afraid that something terrible will happen to their children or that some dreaded catastrophe
will befall them. When they read about a pandemic, they live in fear
that they will catch the illness. Some imagine they have it already.
In many cases, they literally "worry themselves sick."

Catastrophizing doesn't necessarily apply only to life and
death situations or severe illnesses. It can occur in any challenging
situation—for example, leading up to a major exam or a competitive
athletic event. If you worry about your performance or believe that
your competitors are superior, you're putting yourself at a disad-
vantage. Even the smallest seed of doubt can lessen your confidence
and focus and lead to failure or loss. To crowd out any thoughts or
feelings of doubt, focus your mind on success.

De-Catastrophizing

Psychologists and psychiatrists help clients identify and adjust their
counterproductive thought patterns through a technique called

cognitive behavioral therapy (CBT). They teach clients to challenge negative thoughts about themselves and the world and adopt more constructive and rational thought patterns. But you don't need a therapist to shift your thinking. You can do it through conscious effort.

If you have an irrational or overblown fear that's preventing you from doing something that would probably improve your life and add to your enjoyment, move your mind in the opposite direction. Shift your focus past the obstacle you fear to the object of your desire. Get absorbed in what you desire. Know that the subjective thought always produces the objective reality. This attitude will give you confidence and lift your spirits. The infinite power of your subconscious mind is moving on your behalf. It cannot fail. Therefore, you can proceed with confidence.

Stare Down Your Fears

The head of sales for a major multinational corporation confided that when he first began working as a salesperson, he had to walk around the block five or six times before he could get up the courage to call on a customer.

His supervisor was experienced and very perceptive. One day she said to him, "Don't fear the monster hiding behind the door. There is no monster. You're the victim of a false belief."

The supervisor went on to tell him that whenever she felt the first stirrings of a fear, she stood up to it. She stared it in the face, looking it straight in the eye. When she did that, she always found that her fear faded and shrank into insignificance.

From Fear to Desire

A former US Army chaplain named John told me that during World War II, the plane he was in was hit and damaged by anti-aircraft fire. He had to bail out over the mountains of New Guinea and found himself deep in the jungle. Of course, he was frightened, but he knew the difference between rational and irrational fear. He was also aware that irrational fear could easily trigger panic or hopelessness, either of which would be counterproductive.

He decided he'd be wise to calm his growing fear immediately. He began to talk to himself, saying, "John, you can't surrender to your fear. Your fear is just a desire for safety, security, and escape."

He stood in the center of a small clearing and calmed his breathing. He pushed away the first symptoms of panic. As soon as he felt more relaxed, he began to claim, "Infinite intelligence, which guides the planets in their courses, is now leading and guiding me out of this jungle to safety." He kept repeating this out loud to himself.

"Suddenly," John told me, "I felt something start to stir inside me. It was a mood of confidence and faith. I was drawn to one side of the clearing. There I found the faint trace of a path, and I began to walk. Two days later, I came upon a small village where the people were friendly. They fed me, then took me to the edge of the jungle, where a rescue plane picked me up."

John's changed mental attitude saved him. His confidence and trust in the subjective wisdom and power within him delivered the solution to his problem.

He added, "If I had started to bemoan my fate and indulge my fears, the monster fear would have conquered me. I probably would have died of fear and starvation."

They Plotted Against Him

During a world lecture tour, I had a two-hour conversation with a prominent government official in one of the countries I visited. I found that this man had a deep sense of inner peace and serenity. He said that although he is constantly showered with abuse by newspapers that support the opposition party, he never lets it disturb him. His practice is to sit still for fifteen minutes in the morning and realize that in the center of himself is a deep, still ocean of peace. Meditating in this way, he generates tremendous power, which overcomes all sorts of difficulties and fears.

A few months earlier, he had received a midnight call from a panicky colleague. According to his coworker, a group of people were plotting against him. They intended to overthrow his administration by force, with help from dissident elements of the country's armed forces.

In reply, the official told his colleague, "I am going to sleep now in perfect peace. We can discuss this tomorrow morning at ten o'clock."

As he explained to me, "I know that no negative thought can ever manifest itself unless I emotionalize the thought and accept it mentally. I refused to entertain their suggestion of fear. Therefore, no harm could come to me unless I allowed it."

Notice how calm he was, how cool, how serene. He didn't panic. He had no need to panic. At his center was still water, an ocean of peace.

Overcome Your Fear

Now it's your turn. Identify your biggest self-limiting fear. Are you afraid of asking a certain person on a date? Trying out for a position on a sports team? Auditioning for a part in a play? Delivering a presentation? Are you afraid of taking a risk? Describe your fear and what it's preventing you from doing:

- My fear is _____
- It is preventing me from _____

Now, envision your life after overcoming your fear. Describe how your life is different and better after you've overcome your fear and gotten what you wanted.

Write a brief affirmation expressing your confidence and your gratitude for having accomplished your goal (focus on the opposite of what you fear).

Repeat your affirmation several times daily, replaying the vision of how your life is different and better upon achieving your goal. Continue until your fear has been entirely replaced with confidence.

Tell your own story of how you overcame your fear.

CHAPTER 9
Excel at School and Work

As water by cooling and condensation becomes ice,
so thought by condensation assumes physical form.
Everything in the universe is thought in material form.
—Paramahansa Yogananda, Spiritual Teacher

We all want to excel in our studies and our careers. For some, it comes easy. Others struggle, putting forth great effort over long hours and still not achieving the same level of success as their less diligent but more gifted counterparts. Certainly, some people have a genetic advantage—their brains function at a higher level, or they're born with some awesome talent. But even at the low end of the spectrum, every human being has incredible potential. And, thanks to neuroplasticity (the brain's ability to change), our brains are capable of growing neurons and developing new neural networks as we learn.

In other words, we all have the capacity to become smarter and better at whatever we choose to do. Each of us also has access to an infinite storehouse of knowledge and wisdom by way of our subconscious minds.

So what's standing in the way of those of us who aren't achieving our full potential at school or work? What's preventing us from achieving the level of success we're capable of? Is it other people? Is it circumstances beyond our control, like lack of money or influence—our socioeconomic status? No. It is usually something within. As much as we like to deny it, what's usually holding us back is our attitude or mindset, our lack of determination or stick-to-itiveness.

If you understand the power of the subconscious mind, you know that external circumstances or conditions cannot limit our success, because through the power of our subconscious minds, we create our own external circumstances. And other people can't hold us back because they can't control what we think—we have total control over our own thoughts and emotions. Therefore, the only thing that can possibly hold us back is us.

Further proof that attitude or mindset is the key to success comes from the many stories of people who had everything going against them and were able to rise above it all and accomplish great things—people like Oprah Winfrey, who was born into poverty; Richard Branson, who has dyslexia; and J. K. Rowling, who survived as a single mother living on government welfare and had her *Harry Potter* manuscript rejected twelve times before achieving phenomenal success.

Maybe they got a lucky break at some point in their careers, but they didn't get the break by sitting on their hands and waiting for it to happen. They continued to pursue their goals, and when the lucky breaks came along, they capitalized on them. As legendary golfer Gary Player often said, "The more I practice, the luckier I get."

I'm also amazed by immigrants who come to the United States with little more than the clothes on their backs and manage somehow to build profitable businesses, while many people born in the

US, who have easy access to food, housing, and education, blame a lack of opportunity for their lack of progress. It is clearly attitude that separates the successful immigrant from the destitute natural-born citizen. And attitude is a choice.

From Failing Grades to Straight As

Sixteen-year-old Todd told me, "I'm failing everything. I don't know why. I guess I'm just stupid. Maybe I'd better drop out of school before I flunk out."

As we talked further, I discovered that the only thing wrong with Todd was his attitude. He felt indifferent toward his studies and resentful toward some of his teachers and fellow students.

I taught him how to use his subconscious mind to succeed in his studies. He began to affirm certain truths several times a day, particularly at night just before falling asleep and first thing after waking in the morning. He affirmed as follows:

My subconscious mind is a storehouse of memory. It retains everything I read and everything my teachers present. I have a perfect memory. The infinite intelligence of my subconscious mind constantly reveals to me everything I need to know on all my examinations, whether written or oral. I radiate love and goodwill to all my teachers and fellow students. I sincerely wish them success and all good things.

While repeating this affirmation, Todd would imagine his teachers and parents congratulating him on his success in his studies. He would also imagine his fellow students looking up to him and asking him for help with their assignments.

Within a few weeks, Todd was beginning to excel in his classes. He progressed from nearly failing to being a straight-A student. His parents and his teachers, awestruck by his incredible transformation, congratulated him on his diligence and intelligence, and he quickly earned the respect of his fellow students.

Define Success

Success at school or work depends on how you envision it. Do you measure success at school in terms of grades, pleasing your teachers, pleasing your parents, mastery of the subject matter, being the head of your class, or something else? At work, do you measure success by your hourly pay or salary, being voted employee of the month, pleasing customers, pleasing your supervisor, excelling at your job, coming up with great ideas, or something else?

Spend a few minutes describing what it means to you to be successful at school or work.

Of course, success in life is bigger than success at school or work. In the larger scheme of things, success is measured by a collection of intangibles—serenity, harmony, integrity, compassion, curiosity, happiness, enthusiasm, generosity, and so on. All these intangibles are products of your mind, and they're mostly emotions. They're part of your deeper self, and they all contribute to your tangible and intangible success.

To achieve higher levels of success at school and work, nurture the deeper qualities in you that drive your success. For example, be curious, enthusiastic, and joyful about your schoolwork. When dealing with coworkers and customers at work, be compassionate, understanding, and forgiving. When you think about school or work, envision yourself as an embodiment of those deeper, positive qualities. As your vision is passed to your subconscious mind and is reflected in your physical world, all those qualities will be translated into higher levels of achievement and greater levels of success.

The Three Steps to Success

The secret to success is finding the sweet spot or, as some people like to say, "finding one's calling." The sweet spot is the point at which your interests and talents meet a strong need or demand for what you have to offer; for example, you have a passion for performing along with musical talents and there's a strong demand for that form of entertainment. Or you're mechanically inclined, you love to tinker with engines, and there's a strong demand for auto mechanics in your area.

When you find something you love and are good at, and there's a strong demand for what you have to offer, you can't help but be successful. And it'll seem easy to you. The following sections lead you through the three-step process to finding your sweet spot.

Step 1: Discover what you love to do.

The vital first step to success is to find out what you love to do. Unless you love your work, you can't possibly consider yourself successful at it, even if all the rest of the world hails you as a great success. Loving your work, you have a deep desire to carry it out. If someone is drawn to become a psychiatrist, it is not enough for her to get a diploma and hang it on the wall. She will want to keep up with the field, attend conventions, and continue studying the mind and its workings. She will visit other clinics and pore over the latest scientific journals. In other words, she will work to keep herself

informed in the most advanced methods of alleviating mental suffering, because she's passionate about it.

But what if, as you read these words, you find yourself thinking,
"I can't take the first step, because I don't know what I want to do.
How on earth do I find a field of endeavor that I will love?" The
answer to that question is this: Consult your subconscious mind,
which knows more about you and about everything than your conscious mind can imagine. Every day, several times daily, repeat the
following affirmation:

The infinite intelligence of my subconscious mind reveals to
me my true place in life.

Repeat this affirmation quietly, positively, and lovingly to your
deeper mind with the certainty that it has the answer. As you persist with confidence and certainty, the answer will come to you as a
feeling, a hunch, or a tendency in a certain direction. It will come to
you clearly and in peace, and as an inner silent awareness.

Step 2: Discover what you're really good at.

Every person is born with talents and potential to excel in one or
more fields of endeavor. Some have more academic potential, others are more mechanically or athletically inclined, and others are
born leaders. And over the course of their lives, everyone acquires
knowledge and skills through study and experience. The sum total
of an individual's personality, knowledge, experience, talents, and
skills typically makes that individual uniquely qualified for a specific mission or career.

People who know what they love and what they're really good
at usually discover it much easier to find their path to success, so

I encourage you to get to know yourself. Start your personal self-examination by responding to the following prompts:

- What subjects do you excel in at school?
- Which extracurricular activities have you participated in and enjoyed?
- List your favorite hobbies and pastimes.
- What skills or talents do you have?
- What are you qualified enough to teach others to do?
- What have others told you you're good at or would be good at doing?
- What is your greatest accomplishment?
- Are you a leader or a follower?
- Are you good at solving problems?
- If you could have any job or business you wanted, what would it be?

Remember that everything you've done in the past prepares you for your future, even mistakes you've made and learned from. A close examination of your past and of the deeper you is likely to reveal a clear path to your future.

Step 3: Identify a need.

Doing what you love to do and are great at doing isn't enough. Your life's work must also serve the needs of others. It must fulfill a demand. It must improve the lives of others in some way. To give what you have to offer, others must be ready to receive it, thereby completing the circuit and allowing your contributions to flow freely, multiply, and deliver an abundant return on your personal investment. Your idea must go forth with the purpose of serving the world. It will then come back to you magnified and full of blessings. If you work only for your own benefit, you do not complete this essential circuit.

Those who are most successful in the world have adopted a servant mentality. They seek to serve the needs of others and improve their lives. There is an enormous contrast between this attitude of mind and that of someone who wants only to "make a living" or just "get by." Getting by is not true success. People's motives must be greater, nobler, and more altruistic. They must serve others, thereby meeting a demand for what they have to offer.

Look at what you love to do and what you're great at doing in the context of what's needed in the world. Based on your conscious examination of these three factors—what you love to do, what you're good at doing, and what's needed or is in high demand—start brainstorming ideas for jobs, careers, and businesses that may be a good fit for you.

Now, engage your subconscious mind to reveal the path to your future. Several times daily repeat the following affirmation:

> I know what I love to do and what I'm perfectly suited to do. There is a strong need for my unique blend of talents, skills, knowledge, and experience. My subconscious mind reveals the perfect opportunities for me, and I am filled with gratitude for its wisdom and guidance.

Over time, your subconscious mind will deliver the answer. The answer may be given through a sudden realization, a chance meeting with a stranger, a presenter at your school's career day, something a teacher reveals to you, something you see on the internet, or some other form of communication. When you receive the answer, write it down.

True Success

At this point, you may be thinking, "What about that guy on the news who made hundreds of millions of dollars from shady stock deals? He's a huge success, and he has no concerns about making the world a better place."

Such cases are all too common, but we must be careful to understand them for what they are. Someone may seem to succeed for a while, but money obtained by fraudulent means tends to disappear. Even if it doesn't, when we steal from others, we steal from ourselves. The attitude of lack and limitation that led to our criminal behavior manifests itself in other ways as well—in our body, our home life, our relationships with others.

What we think and feel, we create. We create what we believe. Even though someone may have accumulated a fortune fraudulently, he's not successful. There's no success without peace of mind. What good is a person's accumulated wealth if he's plagued by guilt, sleepless nights, illness, and broken relationships? He may appear happy and well-adjusted on the outside, while he's being torn up inside.

I once met a professional criminal in London who told me of his exploits. He had amassed a large fortune that allowed him to live in luxury in his house outside London and his summer home in France. In luxury, yes, but not in comfort. He was in constant dread of being arrested by Scotland Yard. He had many inner disorders that were undoubtedly caused by his constant fear and deep-seated guilt. He knew he had done wrong. This deep sense of guilt attracted all kinds of trouble to him.

Later, I heard that he had voluntarily turned himself in to the police and had served a prison sentence. After his release from prison, he sought psychological and spiritual counsel and became transformed. He went to work and became an honest, law-abiding citizen. He found what he loved to do and was happy.

A successful person loves her work and expresses herself fully. Success is contingent upon a higher ideal than the mere accumulation of riches. The person of success is the person who possesses great psychological and spiritual understanding. Many of the great business leaders of today depend upon the correct use of their subconscious minds for their success. They cultivate the ability to see an upcoming project as if it were already complete. Having seen and felt the fulfillment of their vision, their subconscious minds bring about its realization. If you imagine an objective clearly, you will be provided with the necessities, in ways you may never have imagined, through the wonder-working power of your subconscious mind.

In considering the three steps to success, never forget the underlying power of the creative forces of your subconscious mind. This is the energy behind all the steps in any plan of action. Your thought is creative. Thought fused with positive feeling becomes a mental certainty, which is ultimately brought to fruition in the physical world.

Once you understand that you possess a mighty force within you that is capable of bringing to pass all your desires, you gain both confidence and a sense of peace. Whatever your field of endeavor may be, you should learn the laws of your subconscious mind. When you know how to apply the powers of your mind and when you are expressing yourself fully and giving of your talents to others, you are on the sure path to true success. When you have the infinite intelligence and power of universal consciousness working for you, nothing can stand between you and success.

Consult Your Board of Directors

Some years ago, I gave a lecture to a group of business executives on the powers of imagination and the subconscious mind. In the course of the lecture, I described how the great German poet Goethe used his imagination wisely when confronted with difficulties and predicaments.

According to Goethe 's biographers, he was accustomed to spending many hours quietly in imaginary conversations. He would imagine one of his friends sitting across from him, giving him correct answers to all his questions. In other words, if he were concerned over any problems, he imagined his friend giving him the perfect solution, accompanied with his usual gestures and tonal qualities of the voice. He made the entire imaginary scene as real and as vivid as possible.

One of the people present at this lecture was a young stockbroker. She proceeded to adopt Goethe's technique. She began to have imaginary conversations with a multimillionaire investor who knew her and had once congratulated her on her wise and sound judgment in recommending stocks. She dramatized this imaginary conversation until she had psychologically fixed it as a form of belief in her mind.

This broker's internal conversations and controlled imagination certainly agreed with her aim, which was to make sound investments for her clients. Her main purpose in life was to make money for her clients and to see them prosper financially by her wise counsel. She relied on her subconscious mind over the course of her career and was a brilliant success in her field.

Making "Success" Your Mantra

Many prominent business executives quietly repeat the word *success* over and over many times a day until they feel that their success is certain. They know that every successful venture begins as an idea in someone's mind. Therefore, success itself begins as an idea. The idea contains all the essential elements of success.

Follow their lead. Several times throughout the day, repeat the word *success* with conviction and certainty. Your subconscious mind will accept it as true of you, and you will be under a subconscious compulsion to succeed. You will be compelled to express your impressions, ideas, and convictions.

Imagine yourself as the person you want to be, doing what you want to do, possessing the things you long to possess, and living the life you dreamed of. Be creative. In your mind, participate in the reality of the success you imagine. Make a habit of it. Go to sleep feeling successful every night and perfectly satisfied, and you will eventually succeed in implanting the idea of success in your subconscious mind. Believe you were born to succeed, and wonders will happen.

CHAPTER 10

Get Others to Respect You

Our greatest human adventure is the evolution of consciousness. We are in this life to enlarge the soul, liberate the spirit, and light up the brain.

—Tom Robbins, American Novelist

Everyone wants to be respected by others. We want the respect of our parents, teachers, supervisors, and, perhaps most, our peers. Of course, we can't control what people think of us and how they treat us, but we can influence their opinion. It all begins with self-respect. As the ancient Chinese philosopher Confucius once said, "Respect yourself and others will respect you." While that statement isn't entirely true, what is true is that getting others to respect you starts with respecting yourself.

But it doesn't end there.

People won't always respect you just because you respect yourself. You also need to show respect to others who deserve it, and you need to demonstrate that you're deserving of respect with your words and actions. This chapter helps you master the fundamentals of getting others to respect you.

Remember that much of what's required to earn the respect of others involves changing yourself through the power of your conscious and subconscious minds. Changes occur first internally, with modifications in thinking and emotion. Internal changes are then expressed externally in choices and behaviors. And finally, the internal and external changes become manifest in how the physical world, including the people you interact with, respond to the new you.

Build Positive Self-Esteem

An essential ingredient of self-respect is self-esteem, which is entirely a product of the mind. We choose what we think and feel about ourselves. However, positive self-esteem is often diminished or destroyed in a child who's neglected or abused physically or emotionally. If you're raised to think that you're unloved or unlovable, if you're not challenged in ways that help you build confidence, if you're not praised for your accomplishments, or if you're constantly criticized, you're likely to grow up lacking self-esteem.

Self-esteem is buried deep in our subconscious minds. We don't give it much thought, but it subtly, yet powerfully, controls our lives. High self-esteem gives us the confidence and courage to pursue prosperity, happiness, and self-fulfillment. Low self-esteem fills us with fear and uncertainty, which limit every aspect of our lives— our education, career, relationships, and overall enjoyment of life.

Here are seven ways to start building self-esteem:

1. Repeat positive affirmations daily, such as this one: *I am proud of myself, my talents, and my achievements.*
2. Commit to continuing education. Always be in the process of developing new knowledge, understanding, and skills.

3. Accept compliments, even if they make you feel uncomfortable. You may even want to write them down and use them in your affirmations.

4. Forgive yourself. Learn from your mistakes, and then let them go. You can't undo something bad you did in the past, but you can learn from it.

5. Accept criticism, learn from it, and then let it go. The only good that comes from the criticism you receive is an opportunity for improvement. Don't keep playing the criticism over in your mind or resent the source of that criticism.

6. List your strengths and positive qualities in the context of an area you're struggling with, such as school, employment, or relationships. For example, if you didn't get hired for a job you really wanted and applied for, write a list of qualities that make you an ideal candidate for the job—for example, you're always on time, committed to excellence, and customer oriented.

7. If you have a habit of comparing yourself to others, stop it. Remind yourself that if two people were exactly the same, the world wouldn't need one of them. You're needed in the world for the unique qualities you have.

Be Assertive

Assertiveness is a reflection of confidence. It involves telling people what you think, like, and accept firmly and politely. By being assertive, you subtly convey that you respect yourself and expect others to respect you.

To find out whether you struggle with being assertive, make a mental note of each of the following statements that pertains to you:

- You often avoid confrontation instead of resolving disagreements or solving problems.
- You frequently defer to others without expressing your preference. For example, instead of expressing your desire to eat at a certain restaurant, you say something like, "Whatever you want is fine."
- You often leave decisions up to others instead of expressing or defending your opinion.
- You dismiss your own opinion with statements such as "Whatever" and "I don't care."
- You're reluctant to tell others "no" when they ask you to do something for them. Or, worse, people around you assume that you'll do favors for them without even showing you the courtesy of asking.
- You're afraid that if you express your opinion, people will reject you or not like you.
- You're so focused on serving the needs of others that your needs are neglected.
- You say "sorry" to others far more than they say "sorry" to you.

Don't confuse assertiveness with aggressiveness. You can express your opinion and your preferences firmly and politely without raising your voice or using threatening gestures.

Here are a few suggestions that may help you become more assertive:

- Be honest, especially about how you feel, what you need, and what you like.
- Establish clear boundaries. Clarify what you're willing to do and what you won't do.

- Stand your ground. People will challenge your boundaries. Remind yourself and them what your limits are and resist anyone's attempts to push your limits.
- Be proactive in resolving problems and disagreements.
- Communicate in simple, direct language that leaves no room for interpretation. To be less confrontational, you can start your statements with "I," but still be direct; for example, you may say something like, "I feel as though I'm being used."
- Put your needs first. When you're on an airplane, the flight attendant instructs you that if oxygen masks are required, put yours on first before helping a child or someone else with theirs. Before you can help others meet their needs, your needs must be met. Make sure they are. Being sure that your needs are met is not selfish.

Be Open-Minded

Although expressing your opinions clearly and firmly is important, equally important is listening to others and being prepared to change what you think when provided with new information or different perspectives. Being close-minded or stubborn is a sign of disrespect to others. You're showing that you don't care what others think and perhaps aren't even willing to listen to why they think what they think.

A good rule of thumb is to listen twice as much as you talk. We have two ears and only one mouth for a reason. Before arguing a point, fully understand the other person's position. Ask questions to clear up any misunderstanding. When you think you understand the person's position, repeat it back to them in your own words so that they have an opportunity to correct any misunderstanding. People often engage in arguments simply because they have an incorrect understanding of each other's position.

Another good rule of thumb is to check the facts. Don't assume that what you think or what the other person is telling you is true. If you have any doubt, gather additional information. You may even want to gather input from other people. Sometimes both parties engaged in a disagreement are wrong, and an objective third-party perspective can resolve the conflict.

Resolve Disagreements Rationally

As humans, we're prone to disagreement because we have different perspectives and ways of thinking. This isn't necessarily bad. After all, sometimes we're wrong and need to be corrected. Sometimes the other person is wrong. And sometimes, new perspectives, thoughts, and understandings arise through the process of resolving conflict.

Disagreements also provide us with opportunities to earn (or lose) respect. We can lose respect by getting angry, blaming others, criticizing the other person behind her back, giving the other person the silent treatment, or even avoiding the conflict altogether hoping the problem will go away.

To earn respect, confront the other person politely and discuss the issue. If you have conflicting opinions, listen carefully to the other person and ask questions so that you fully understand that person's position before presenting yours. If you're facing a problem and disagree over the solution, try to take a collaborative approach. Don't get caught up in the blame game. Look past any personality conflict and any disagreement over who might have caused the problem to focus on possible solutions. Analyze the problem together, brainstorm solutions, and pick the one that seems most promising.

Even after a rational discussion, you may not reach an agreement, but discussion conducted in the spirit of increasing understanding and resolving differences often leads to mutual respect. The other person will likely respect you more than before simply because you demonstrated your integrity by confronting them in a constructive way and discussing the issue openly.

Resist Peer Pressure

As much as we desire to be unique individuals, we humans typically have a strong desire to fit in, so most of us are very susceptible to peer pressure. However, while going along with the crowd may make us feel accepted in the short term, it can lead to a long-term loss of respect, especially if the peer pressure encourages us to engage in unethical activities or bad behaviors—abusing alcohol or drugs, vandalizing property, shoplifting, bullying, and so on.

To earn the respect of others, live according to a strict code of conduct. A good place to start is with the Golden Rule—treat others as you would like to be treated. Another good rule of thumb is to obey the law. By having a code of conduct in place, you're less likely to be persuaded to engage in illegal or unethical activities by someone who's influential or persuasive.

If you feel pressured to do something that doesn't feel right to you, take the following steps to resist the pressure:

1. Take time to breathe and analyze the situation. Ask whether what you're being pressured to do aligns with your code of conduct. Consider the consequences of giving in to the peer pressure.

2. Politely decline the offer to do something wrong. You don't have to give a reason. Just say something like, "No thanks," or "I'd really prefer not to."

3. Suggest a different activity, make an excuse to leave the situation, or simply walk away. However, if someone is being bullied or physically threatened, you may need to intervene by telling the perpetrator to stop or contacting a person in authority and reporting the incident.

Avoid getting into an argument with the person who's trying to persuade you to do wrong. Telling them that what they're doing is wrong may be too confrontational. Instead, use "I" phrases to communicate your position. For example, instead of saying something like, "You're going to get in trouble for painting graffiti on that wall," say something like, "I'm not going to vandalize other people's property. I'm going to the park to play ball instead."

When you stand up for what you believe is right, most people will respect you. And if they don't, then you're probably better off without them in your life.

Accept Criticism Gracefully

How you respond to criticism can contribute to how much people respect you. If you typically respond by becoming defensive and rejecting the criticism outright or, perhaps worse, blaming others for something you did or failed to do, people will generally think less highly of you. However, if you listen to the criticism and carefully consider it, even if you decide that what you're being told about yourself is wrong, people will respect you.

Here are a few suggestions for accepting criticism gracefully:

- Instead of looking at criticism as blame or as a personal attack against you, view it as an opportunity to improve.
- Listen to the criticism you receive. Ask questions if you don't fully understand what you're being told.
- Consider the truth and relevance of the criticism. We often have a knee-jerk reaction to criticism (rejecting it outright) and only later realize that the criticism was warranted. Ask yourself whether what you're being told is accurate. Did you make a mistake? Is there room for improvement?
- If you disagree with the criticism, politely explain the situation from your perspective. Take the approach of trying to improve mutual understanding and solve a problem instead of getting defensive or blaming others.
- If the person criticizing you is only pointing out a mistake you made or some shortcoming they think you have, without giving you any suggestions for how to correct it, ask what they think you can do to improve. Ask for constructive criticism.
- If you were at fault, own it. Being accountable and trying to improve will earn the respect of others.

Embrace Your Vulnerability

Vulnerability is the quality of being susceptible to feeling hurt. Many people equate it with weakness, but it's more like sensitivity, which is a strength. Being vulnerable means that you're sensitive to both pain and pleasure, you're confident and secure, and you're honest about yourself—you're aware that you're not perfect. Vulnerability is also at the core of many other qualities that people respect, such as modesty, humility, openness, and affection.

Here are some ways to show vulnerability:

- Tell the truth, especially the truth about yourself. Honesty is a big part of vulnerability.
- Admit your mistakes.
- Give credit to others who've earned it. Be willing to share your success.
- Be self-effacing. Don't try to draw attention to yourself. Admit and even laugh at your own imperfections. Being self-effacing is a great way to be funny without the risk of hurting other people's feelings. However, don't get into the habit of constantly putting yourself down.
- Share the challenges and problems you're struggling with in your own life.
- Express your feelings honestly and openly.
- Share your dreams and what you're passionate about.

When showing vulnerability, be careful not to overshare. Sharing too much information (TMI) can be just as bad, if not worse, than not sharing enough. Be especially careful about sharing too much information in any documented form, such as via social media, email, or texts. Also, be selective when showing vulnerability. Generally, you'll want to show your vulnerability more to people you know and trust in safer (more private) settings. You can still show vulnerability in more public settings, such as your school and workplace, but "gauge the room"—calibrate what and how much you want to reveal about yourself based on the situation and the people present.

Keep in mind that what you share is entirely your choice. You have a right to privacy. Share only what you're comfortable sharing with the people you choose to share it with. As you gain confidence in yourself and trust in others, you'll feel more comfortable exposing your vulnerabilities.

Make Improvements, Not Excuses

One of the best ways to earn respect is to not make excuses for mistakes you've made. Accept responsibility, repair any damage, and do your best to avoid making the same mistake in the future.

Don't confuse an explanation with an excuse. An explanation of what caused a problem or made you behave in a certain way or say the wrong thing helps you and others understand the situation and address it effectively. An excuse, on the other hand, is an attempt to avoid responsibility.

Even if you're entirely blameless, presenting an excuse instead of a solution does little, if anything, to fix the problem or prevent it from happening again. For example, I once had an associate at an auto parts store sell me the wrong catalytic converter for my car. I had told him the correct year, make, and model number of my car, so I should have received the correct part. When I tried to return the part later, a different associate was working behind the counter. He informed me that they didn't have the correct part in stock.

When he refunded my money for the wrong part, he subtracted a 15 percent restocking fee. I explained that I was sold the wrong part and therefore shouldn't have to pay the restocking fee, and he replied, "*I* didn't sell you the wrong part!" I explained further that even though he wasn't personally responsible, a store representative was, and I shouldn't be penalized for the store's error. He provided the full refund.

The point here is that even if you're not personally responsible for a mistake, you'll have a better outcome by spending less time and effort avoiding responsibility and more time finding a solution or making improvements to avoid similar mistakes in the future. The second associate at the store would have been wise to consult a manager, who could identify and correct the underlying reason why I was sold the wrong part. Perhaps the other salesperson needed additional training or the information they had about the part needed to be corrected in their system.

In any event, if you seek ways to correct mistakes and improve, you'll have better outcomes and earn more respect.

CHAPTER 11

Make Friends and Nurture Friendships

As we grow in our consciousness, there will be more compassion and more love, and then the barriers between people, between religions, between nations will begin to fall.
—RAM DASS, SPIRITUAL TEACHER

Friends enrich your life. Good friends increase your sense of belonging, give your life purpose, enhance your enjoyment of life, reduce stress, boost your self-esteem, help you cope with problems, and encourage you when you're facing challenges in your life. Close friendships even improve health, reducing risks of depression, high blood pressure, heart attack, stroke, and other health conditions, especially when friends engage in healthy activities together.

Unfortunately, building and maintaining enjoyable, constructive friendships can be a challenge. Some people, the social butterflies among us, have no trouble making friends, but the loners and less popular of us often struggle in this area of our lives. If you have trouble making and keeping good friends, that's about to change.

Know What You Want in a Friend

Attracting the right people into your life is easy when you have the power of your subconscious mind working for you. You simply tell your subconscious mind that you're looking for friends and provide some selection guidelines. The challenge is to figure out what you value in a friend. What qualities or characteristics are you looking for?

Here's a list of qualities to consider:

- Shares your interests
- Clicks with your personality (a good match)
- Accepts you as you are
- Has your back
- Is honest and open
- Shows compassion
- Has a good sense of humor
- Respects you
- Respects your privacy (doesn't tell secrets)
- Inspires you to be your best self

Imagine your current and future friends, and then write a brief description of what they're like and why you like spending time with them.

Engage Your Subconscious Mind in Your Search

Now that you know consciously what you're looking for in a friendship, enlist the aid of your subconscious mind. Write a brief affirmation, instructing it to attract the right people into your life. Here's an example to use for inspiration:

I love and respect myself and am deserving of love and respect. I am a good friend, and I attract friends easily. Infinite intelligence knows who I am and what I need and draws the right people into my life at the right times. I am grateful for all the wonderful friends I have.

Repeat your affirmation several times daily over the course of one to two weeks. As you recite your affirmation (to yourself or aloud), envision yourself with one or more friends doing what you love to do together. Try to engage as many of your senses as possible in your imaginary activity—sight, hearing, smell, taste, and touch. At the end of a couple weeks, hand the task over to your subconscious mind trusting that it will attract the perfect candidates for friendship into your life.

Make Friendship a Priority

Many people have trouble making and maintaining friendships because they have other demands, such as school, work, and family responsibilities. I encourage you to make friendship a top priority. Why? Because friendship makes everything else easier and more enjoyable and can enhance success in all areas of your life—academics, athletics, career, family, you name it. If you don't have friends, you're limiting yourself.

Everyone should have at least one best friend, so start there. Who's your bestie or BFF (best friend forever)? Cherish that person. Most people also have several close friends along with some casual friends and acquaintances (people they've met but don't know very well). Stay in touch with your bestie and try to communicate at least once a week, preferably in person. If necessary, schedule time each week to meet. Plan something special once or twice each year to create memories together and deepen your bond.

Make Yourself an Attractive Target

People who complain about not having friends would often find, if they took an honest look at themselves, that they're driving people away instead of attracting them. Without being aware of it, they may come across as insecure, unhappy, or even unkind. If you're often in a bad mood, you're likely to appear unapproachable or not very pleasant to be around.

Take an honest look at yourself. Which of the following statements (if any) pertain to you?

- When talking to others, I often complain about things in my life.
- I say bad things about other people behind their back.
- I talk a lot about myself and rarely ask about the other person I'm talking to.
- I criticize or offer advice even when nobody asked for my opinion.
- I could be described as being too honest.
- I interrupt others when they're talking.
- I often lose interest when someone is telling me something, and when that happens, I stop paying attention to what they're saying.
- I tend to take what people say to me personally and get defensive.
- I don't smile or laugh very much at all.

If you checked most of the boxes, you really can't expect people to feel attracted to you. You're probably driving them away with a negative attitude. People are generally more attracted to those who are living a life of abundance and joy—those who have discovered the power of their subconscious mind and are using it to enrich their lives.

To nurture a more positive attitude, reinforce positive thoughts and reject negative ones. Several times daily over the next two or three weeks, and whenever negative thoughts begin to enter your mind, repeat the following affirmation:

I am an amazing person living in an awesome world populated with wonderful people. Every day is filled with opportunity and abundance, and I find joy in every breath. I smile and greet people and speak with them easily. I wish everyone a life of abundance and joy. I am grateful to be alive.

As you repeat this affirmation, imagine yourself interacting with others in a pleasant manner. Envision the joy on their faces as they interact with you. Think about all the good things in your life—everything you're thankful for.

Forgive

One way people drive others away is by holding a grudge. Being angry or bitter inside shows on the outside, and it's not attractive. Have you ever noticed someone who seems to have a permanent scowl on his face? Have you felt attracted to that person? Nobody wants to be around someone who's bitter and angry all the time. When you forgive others, you set your own mind at ease and you radiate warmth, joy, and acceptance, all of which are attractive qualities.

Forgive yourself for wrongs you have committed and forgive everyone who has ever harmed you in any way. If you've harmed someone in the past, apologize and ask for their forgiveness. Receiving forgiveness can ease your mind too. However, if someone refuses to forgive you, you must still forgive yourself and move on. You can't compel anyone to forgive you.

Here is a simple but effective method to forgive yourself and others. It will work wonders in your life as you practice it. Quiet your mind, relax, and let go. Think of universal love flowing through you and uniting all things as you recite the following affirmation:

I fully and freely forgive myself and [the name of the person who offended you]. I release him [or her] mentally and spiritually. I completely forgive everything connected with the matter in question. I am free, and he [or she] is free. It is a marvelous feeling.

This is my day of general amnesty. I release anybody and everybody who has ever hurt me, and I wish for each and every one health, happiness, peace, and all the blessings of life. I do this freely, joyously, and lovingly.

Whenever you think of the person or persons who hurt you say, "I have released you, and all the blessings of life are yours. I am free and you are free. It is wonderful!"

The great secret of true forgiveness is that once you have forgiven the person, you can stop repeating the affirmation. Whenever the person comes to your mind, or the incident enters your mind, wish the person well, and say, "I wish you peace." Do this as often as the thought enters your mind. You will find that after a few days the thought of the person or experience will return less and less often, until it fades into nothingness.

However, be careful not to fool yourself into thinking that you've forgiven someone when you haven't. Prospectors and jewelers use what is called an acid test to tell if a metal is real gold or an imitation. There is an acid test for forgiveness too. Imagine me telling you something wonderful about a person who has hurt you in some way. If you bristle at hearing the good news about this person, the roots of hatred are still in your subconscious mind, playing havoc with you.

Suppose you had a very painful dental procedure last year and you tell me about it now. If I ask whether you are in pain from it now, you would give me an astonished look and say, "Of course not! I remember the pain, but I don't feel it any longer." Likewise, if you've truly forgiven someone, you will remember the incident but will no longer feel the sting or hurt of it.

Once you understand the creative power of your own mind, you stop blaming other people and factors that are beyond your control for hurting you. You realize that your own thoughts and feelings create your reality. Furthermore, you're aware that externals are not the causes and conditions of your life and your experiences. To think that others can detract from your happiness, that you are the victim of a cruel fate, that you must compete against others to get what you want—all these ideas reveal their destructive nature once you understand that you control your own destiny.

Put Yourself Out There

If you plant the idea of friendship in the fertile soil of your subconscious mind, it will find a way to attract friends to you even if you're living in a remote location off the grid. However, you can facilitate the process by making yourself more accessible. Chances are good that you're already receiving some exposure to potential friends through school, work, and other activities, but you can expand your pool of candidates in the following ways:

- **Attend parties and other social gatherings.** Parties and other social gatherings are great places to meet people you wouldn't otherwise have the opportunity to interact with.

- **Get involved.** Join a club or other organization whose members share an interest or hobby you would like to explore.

- **Take a class.** If you're out of school or being home-schooled, you may be able to find classes in subjects that interest you through a community college, a local organization, or your town's library or community center.

- **Attend and participate in special events.** Check your local newspaper, library, or online community bulletin board for special events, such as concerts, presentations, art festivals, workshops, and competitions.

- **Volunteer.** Contributing your time and talent to a hospital, community center, or not-for-profit organization can help you learn new skills while giving you the opportunity to meet people who share your values.

- **Explore online opportunities:** Social media sites, including Instagram, TikTok, and Meetup provide an easy means to connect with people who share your interests.

- **Introduce yourself to your neighbors.** One of the easiest ways to start meeting people is to get to know your neighbors. Even if they're not people you would consider befriending, they can open the door to meeting others who are more suitable.

When you're putting yourself out there, be careful. Tell a trusted adult about any individual or group you're planning to meet, so they can help you find out more about the person or group and ensure your safety.

Initiate Contact

If you're waiting for others to approach you, you're taking a passive approach to making friends, and you're leaving the choice entirely up to other people. As explained throughout this book, free thought and free choice give you power over the direction and outcome of your life. When you relinquish those freedoms by taking a passive approach, you're giving up your power to direct your life.

When it comes to making friends, take a proactive approach. Seek out people who share your interests and people you admire, introduce yourself, and strike up a conversation. Taking the initiative may feel uncomfortable at first, but the more you do it, the more comfortable you'll feel. At the same time, you're projecting several very attractive qualities, including warmth, compassion, confidence, acceptance, and the joy of meeting someone for the first time.

Remember, not everyone who would make a great friend is going to come to you. You may need to initiate contact.

The Only Way to Have a Friend Is to Be One

Philosopher and poet Ralph Waldo Emerson wrote, "The only way to have a friend is to be one." A friendship is a mutually beneficial relationship, meaning both parties need to benefit for the friendship to survive. You usually don't start a friendship expecting something in return, but it won't last long if either friend doesn't find it rewarding.

As you form friendships, make sure that you're holding up your end of the bargain:

- **Be available.** As a friend, you need to be available, physically and emotionally, when your friend needs you. If you can't find the time, make the time.

- **Be kind.** Demonstrate to your friends that you value them by showing love and respect and looking for ways to make their lives easier and more enjoyable.

- **Listen and observe.** When you're with friends, listen to what they have to say and be sensitive to their body language. You can usually tell just by looking at someone whether they're feeling hurt, lonely, angry, or sad. Don't hesitate to ask if something's wrong, then listen closely to what they tell you.

- **Open up.** Share details about yourself that you may not share with others. Express how you're feeling. If you're struggling with something, ask for advice or help. Being more open is the key to deepening a relationship.

- **Earn trust.** Be responsible, reliable, and punctual. Keep your promises. Don't share secrets. Be loyal. Remember that people will generally trust you at the beginning of a relationship and will continue to do so over the course of the relationship so long as you don't do something that breaks that trust. In other words, trust is yours to lose. It can also be very difficult to restore.

- **Let the little stuff go.** Don't let a person's minor imperfections spoil an otherwise rewarding relationship. Realize that nobody is perfect and look past the minor mistakes and shortcomings to what's truly important in your relationship.

Be Selective

The world population is nearly 8 billion people. You don't need more than a couple hundred friends. My point is that you can afford to be selective, and you should be. Some people will drag you down. Others may lead you astray. You need to choose friends you like and who enable you to be your best self. Sometimes that means ending a friendship so that you have more time and effort to invest in more rewarding relationships.

Don't waste time in unproductive, unfulfilling relationships that can't be fixed. Recognize the signs that a friendship may need to end:

- You're not getting what you need and expect from the friendship.
- Your friend is being a bad influence, and you lack the willpower to resist.
- You've drifted apart. Neither of you makes an effort to maintain the friendship.
- You feel as though you can't be completely honest or that your friend isn't being completely honest with you.
- You no longer have anything in common.
- One of you has done something to break the other's trust, and that trust can't be restored.
- You fight too much about serious issues that never get resolved.

Good friendships are precious, so don't give up on a friendship just because it becomes difficult. Challenges you encounter together can be golden opportunities to deepen your friendship. If you feel that your friendship is fading, consult your subconscious for guidance.

CHAPTER 12

Find Your Soulmate

Don't settle for anybody just to have someone.
Set your standards. What kind of love do you want
to attract? List the qualities you really want in the
relationship. Develop those qualities in yourself and
you will attract a person who has them.
—Louise Hay, Motivational Speaker and Author

All problems in an intimate relationship are caused by a failure to properly understand the functions and powers of the mind. Friction between partners will disappear when each one uses the law of mind correctly. Unified in mind, they remain together and aligned. The contemplation of ideals, the study of the laws of life, the mutual agreement on a common purpose and plan, and the enjoyment of personal freedom bring about a harmonious state of being—that sense of oneness where the two become one.

The relationship discord that results in frustration, disappointment, sadness, and even anger is no different from all other friction that people experience daily. All conflict can be traced directly to a lack of knowledge of the working and interrelationship of the conscious and subconscious mind. The best time to avoid such conflict is before it begins—by attracting the right person to become your partner and engaging the power of the subconscious mind from the very beginning of the relationship.

There's nothing wrong with deciding to get out of a very bad relationship. But why get into it in the first place? In this chapter, you discover how to attract your ideal partner and use the collective power of your subconscious mind to build an amazing intimate relationship in which you both flourish.

The Meaning of Intimacy

The word *intimacy* describes a very close relationship, one in which partners feel free to be themselves and show their vulnerability in safety, knowing that their partner will keep their secrets and not use sensitive information to harm them. Intimacy enables two people to become closer than otherwise possible and to flourish and fully express themselves without worry of painful repercussions.

To be genuine, an intimate relationship must begin on a solid foundation of love. It must be of the heart. Honesty, sincerity, kindness, and integrity are all aspects of love. Each partner should be perfectly honest and sincere with the other. It is not a true union when people enter a relationship to boost their own ego or because they want to share the other person's money or benefit from that person's connections. This indicates a lack of sincerity, honesty, and true love. A relationship based solely on serving one's own self-interests is a farce, a sham, and a masquerade.

If someone says, "I am tired of working two jobs. I need a partner to help with the bills," their major premise is false. That person isn't using the laws of mind correctly. An individual's security depends not on someone else but on the individual's own knowledge of the interaction of the conscious and subconscious mind and its application.

Nobody will ever lack for wealth or health if they apply the techniques outlined in the chapters of this book. A person's wealth can come independent of a partner, parents, or anyone else. Nobody should depend on another person for health, peace, joy, inspiration, guidance, love, wealth, security, happiness, or anything else in the world. Security and peace of mind come from the knowledge of the powers within and from the constant and consistent use of universal laws applied in constructive ways.

Imagine Your Soulmate

Spend a few minutes thinking about the qualities of your ideal companion—physical, intellectual, emotional, and so on. Imagine, then briefly describe the person you envision and your relationship together.

Attract Your Ideal Partner

Assuming you read the earlier chapters, you're acquainted with the way your subconscious mind works. You know that whatever you impress upon it will be experienced in your physical world. Begin now to impress upon your subconscious mind the qualities and characteristics you desire in a partner.

Here's an effective technique: Sit down at night in a comfortable chair (or lie in bed), close your eyes, let go, relax the body, become very quiet, passive, and receptive. Talk to your subconscious mind and say this to it:

Join me with my soulmate—a person who is honest, sincere, loyal, faithful, peaceful, happy, and prosperous. These qualities that I admire are sinking down into my subconscious mind now. As I dwell upon these characteristics, they become a part of me and are embodied subconsciously.

I know that there is an irresistible law of attraction and that I attract to me the perfect partner according to my subconscious belief. I attract that which I hold true in my subconscious mind.

I know I can contribute to his/her peace and happiness. He/She loves my ideals, and I love his/her ideals. He/She does not want to make me over; neither do I want to make him/her over. We live in mutual love, freedom, and respect.

Practice this process of engaging your subconscious mind in the search for your soulmate. (Feel free to edit the affirmation to more accurately reflect the qualities you're looking for in your ideal partner.) Then you will have the joy of attracting to you the individual possessing the qualities and characteristics you mentally dwelled upon. Your subconscious intelligence will open a pathway whereby both of you will meet, according to the irresistible and changeless flow of your own subconscious mind. Have a keen desire to give the best that is in you of love, devotion, and cooperation. Be receptive to this gift of love, which you have given to your subconscious mind.

Here's another affirmation that's effective for finding a soulmate:

I now attract the ideal companion who is in complete accord with me. The foundation of this union is universal love flowing through two people who are blended to perfection. I know

I can give to my companion love, light, peace, and joy. I can make my partner's life full, complete, and wonderful.

I now decree that he/she possesses the following qualities and attributes: honesty, integrity, passion, sensitivity, and generosity. He/She is peaceful, happy, patient, kind, and confident. We are irresistibly attracted to each other. Only that which belongs to love, truth, and beauty can enter my experience. I accept my ideal companion now.

As you think quietly and with deep interest on the qualities that you admire in the companion you seek, you will build the mental equivalent. Then, the deeper currents of your subconscious mind will bring the two of you together in divine order.

No Need for a Third Mistake

Sheila, a woman with many years of experience as an administrator, said to me, "I have had three husbands and all three have been passive and submissive. They all depended on me to make all decisions and manage everything. Why do I attract such men?"

I asked her if she had known before getting married the second time that her prospective husband had a similar character to her first husband.

"Of course not," she said emphatically. "If I had known that he was such a pushover, I wouldn't have had anything to do with him. And the same goes for my third."

Sheila's trouble did not lie with the men she married. It was a result of her own personality. She was a very assertive person with a strong need to control every situation she found herself in. On one level she wanted a partner who would be submissive and passive so that she could play the dominant role. At the same time, her deeper need was for a partner who would be her equal.

Her subconscious picture attracted to her the sort of man that she subjectively wanted, but once she found one, she discovered that he did not meet her real needs. She had to learn to break this pattern by changing what she was subconsciously asking for.

Sheila finally learned a simple truth. When you're certain you can have your ideal partner, you naturally draw that person into your life.

To break the old subconscious pattern and attract to herself the ideal mate, Sheila used the following affirmation:

I am building into my mentality the type of man I deeply desire. The man I attract for a husband is strong, powerful, loving, successful, honest, loyal, and faithful. He finds love and happiness with me. I love to follow where he leads.

I know he wants me, and I want him. I am honest, sincere, loving, and kind. I have wonderful gifts to offer him. They are goodwill, a joyous heart, and a healthy body. He offers me the same. It is mutual. I give and I receive.

Divine intelligence knows where this man is. The deeper wisdom of my subconscious mind is now bringing both of us together in its own way, and we recognize each other immediately. I release this request to my subconscious mind which knows how to bring my request to pass. I give thanks for the perfect answer.

She repeated this affirmation every day, first thing in the morning and last thing before going to sleep. She affirmed these truths in the certainty that the seeds of thought she was planting in her subconscious mind would grow into the mental equivalent of what she sought, which would ultimately be made real in her physical world.

Several months passed. Sheila had a number of dates and social engagements, but none of the men she met had what she was looking for. She began to wonder if her quest was hopeless. She found herself starting to question, waiver, doubt, and vacillate. At that point, she reminded herself that the infinite intelligence was bringing it to pass in its own way. There was nothing to be concerned about. When she received the final decree in her divorce proceedings, it brought her a great sense of release and mental freedom.

Soon afterward, she took a new position as head administrator in a medical practice. The first day she was on the job, one of the senior physicians came by her office to introduce himself. He had been out of town at a medical conference the day she had interviewed for the position.

The minute he walked in, she knew he was the man she sought. Apparently, he knew it too. He proposed to her within a month. Their subsequent marriage was filled with joy. This physician was not the passive or submissive type. He was strong, confident, and decisive. Well respected in his field, a former college athlete, he was also deeply spiritual.

Sheila received what she requested because she claimed it mentally until the idea reached the point of saturation. In other words, she mentally and emotionally united with her idea, thereby making that idea an inevitability in her life.

Knowing When to End a Relationship

Deciding to end a relationship with a close companion is very much an individual question. There's no general answer that's valid for everyone. In some cases, of course, the couple should have never been together in the first place. In other cases, ending the relationship is not the best course of action. Breaking up may be right for one couple and wrong for another.

In the case of marriage, divorce may be the most honorable and prudent decision. For example, I was once consulted by a woman whose husband beat her and stole from her to support a drug habit. She had been brought up to believe that marriage is sacred and forever and that consequently divorce is immoral. I explained to her that true marriage is of the heart. If two hearts blend harmoniously, lovingly, and sincerely, that is the ideal marriage.

Following this explanation, she knew what to do. She knew in her heart that there is no divine law that compelled her to be intimidated, demoralized, and beaten, simply because someone once said, "I pronounce you husband and wife."

If you're in doubt as to what to do, ask for guidance. Know that there is always an answer and that you will receive it. Follow the lead that comes to you in the silence of your soul. It speaks to you in peace.

Drifting into a Breakup

I once spoke with a young couple who had been together for about a year and were thinking about breaking up. They truly loved one another, but the young man's jealousy and fear of rejection were causing a great deal of tension between the two of them. He expected rejection and believed that she would be unfaithful to him. These thoughts haunted his mind and became an obsession with him.

His mental attitude was one of separation and suspicion. She was unresponsive to him, but this was a result of his own feeling pushing her away. The atmosphere of separation operating through his subconscious mind brought about a condition or action in accordance with the mental pattern behind it. There is a law of action and reaction, or cause and effect. The thought is the action, and the response of the subconscious mind is the reaction.

His girlfriend eventually left—exactly what he had feared and believed she would do. Her leaving was no surprise; he had planted that thought in the fertile soil of his subconscious mind.

When I first met them, they were both full of resentment, fear, suspicion, and anger. These emotions weaken, exhaust, and debilitate. They were experiencing for themselves the universal truth that hate divides and love unites. As we talked and I explained the workings of the conscious and subconscious minds, they began to realize that they were misusing their minds and bringing chaos and misery on themselves.

At my suggestion, they got back together and experimented with affirmation therapy. They began to radiate love, peace, and goodwill to each other. Each one practiced radiating harmony, health, peace, and love to the other and envisioning their ideal relationship. As a result of this sincere effort, and by creating a mental image of their loving relationship, they flourished together as a couple, their relationship growing more beautiful every day.

The Emotionally Needy Partner

Most everyone likes to feel needed, but when someone demands our constant attention, their neediness can become annoying. Often, the reason people are demanding is that they feel neglected. Their legitimate craving for love and affection expresses itself in a way that pushes their loved ones away instead of drawing them closer.

If you're in a close relationship with someone who demands your constant attention, it's usually a sign that the person feels insecure in the relationship. Give that person more attention and show your appreciation. Remind yourself what attracted you to your companion in the first place and praise everything you love about him/her.

Another form of excessive neediness is a desire to make the partner conform to an ideal pattern of behavior the person never agreed to. There are few quicker ways to drive a partner away. Couples must be on their guard not to be always looking for petty faults or errors in each other. Each should give attention to and praise one another's wonderful qualities.

The Brooding Partner

When you're in a long-term relationship, you may encounter a time when you or your partner becomes bitter or resentful over something. Instead of bringing up the issue and resolving it, one or both partners internalize their feelings and brood. Brooding involves thinking deeply about something that makes one unhappy, and it usually shows outwardly in the person's demeanor and facial expression.

Silently resenting your partner is no better than resenting that person demonstratively. It may be even worse, because your partner may have no clue as to the reason for your resentment or how to address whatever wrong you feel you have suffered. In a way, it's like being unfaithful to your partner—unfaithful to your commitment (spoken or unspoken) to love and respect that person.

Brooding is a choice. You can choose to let go of your bitterness, resentment, and anger and try to be considerate, kind, and courteous. You can choose not to be bothered by a difference of opinion or choose to resolve it. Through praise and mental effort, you can work past any antagonism you feel. As you soak your subconscious mind with thoughts of peace, harmony, and love, you will find that you get along better not only with your partner, but with everyone in your life. Assume a harmonious state, and eventually you will find peace and harmony.

Avoid the Big Mistake

It is a great mistake to discuss your relationship problems with neighbors and relatives. Suppose, for example, Crystal tells her friend, "I don't know what I'm going to do about Cole. He hates my mom and is constantly abusive and insulting."

Crystal is degrading and belittling Cole in the eyes of everyone she speaks to. Moreover, as she discusses and dwells upon his shortcomings, she's actually creating these states in her mind. Who is thinking and feeling it? She is! And as you think and feel, so are you.

Besides, relatives usually give the wrong advice. It's usually biased and prejudiced because it's not given in an impersonal way. Any advice you receive that violates the Golden Rule, which is a cosmic law, isn't good or sound.

Remember, no two human beings ever lived under the same roof without strain, clashes of temperament, and periods of hurt. Never display the unhappy side of your intimate relationships to your friends. Keep your quarrels to yourself. Refrain from criticism and condemnation of your partner.

Don't Try to Remake Your Partner

Partners shouldn't try to make each other into second editions of themselves. The tactless attempt to change someone close to you is an affront—a subtle statement that they need to change in order to earn your love. These attempts are always foolish and many times lead to breakups. Attempting to alter someone destroys their pride and self-esteem and often results in making them bitter and resentful.

Adjustments are needed, of course. None of us is perfect, and that holds for marriage partners as well. But if you have a good look inside your own mind and study your own character and behavior, you will find enough shortcomings to keep you busy for the rest of your life. If you think, "I will make him or her over into what I want," you're looking for trouble and asking for misery. You will have to learn the hard way that the only person you have the power to change is yourself.

Four Steps to Harmonious Companionship

After you've found your ideal companion, continue to maintain and deepen your relationship by following these four steps:

1. At the end of each day, forgive one another. Let go of any minor irritations and disappointments.

2. The moment you wake up in the morning, remind yourself that infinite intelligence is guiding you in all your ways. Send out loving thoughts of peace, harmony, and love to your companion, to all members of your family, and to the entire world.

3. When you sit down together for meals, give thanks for the wonderful food, your abundance, and all your blessings. Don't allow problems, worries, or arguments to disrupt the harmony of dining together. Say to your partner, "I appreciate all you are doing, and I radiate love and goodwill to you all day long."

4. Take turns each night affirming your appreciation and admiration for one another. Don't take your partner for granted. Think appreciation and goodwill, rather than condemnation and criticism. To create a rewarding and fulfilling relationship, build it on a foundation of love, beauty, harmony, mutual respect, and the infinite wisdom guiding you.

CHAPTER 13

Have More Fun

*Play touches and stimulates vitality, awakening
the whole person—mind and body, intelligence and
creativity, spontaneity and intuition.*
—Viola Spolin, American Theater Coach

I have a theory that squirrels are the happiest and most productive creatures on the planet. They spend their days gathering, burying, and digging up food, while taking frequent breaks to chase one another playfully through the woods, sometimes leaping fearlessly from treetop to treetop. No other animal I've observed has so much fun. And I have yet to see a squirrel that appears grumpy or dissatisfied.

On the other hand, I observe plenty of people every day blessed with far more creature comforts than squirrels trudging through their lives frustrated, disappointed, anxious, afraid, and depressed. The problem is usually that they're working long, hard hours doing something they hate or are creating (or allowing others to create) drama in their lives that is sapping their energy, stifling their creativity, and smothering their inner joy. Their core problem is that they haven't yet discovered the power of the subconscious mind. As a result, they're just not having much fun.

Fun is defined as "enjoyment, amusement, or lighthearted pleasure," and it is nearly as essential to our health and well-being as physical activity, social engagement, and sleep. Here's a list of ten benefits to having fun:

- Alleviates stress
- Boosts creativity
- Improves social skills
- Helps to heal emotional wounds
- Improves memory
- Restores energy
- Increases productivity
- Enhances your love life
- Improves sleep
- Keeps you feeling young

I'm not suggesting that you become "squirrely" (hyper in an eccentric sort of way), but I do recommend that if you're not smiling and laughing the better part of most days, you put a conscious effort into having more fun. This chapter will help you do just that.

What's Your Idea of Fun?

We often know what we have fun doing, but we do it so rarely that we forget. Spend a few moments in self-exploration to identify activities that you have fun doing. Respond to the following prompts:

- What types of activities do you enjoy most? Board games, video games, sports, hobbies, singing, dancing, reading, watching movies, camping, collecting (cards, coins, stamps, toys), solving mysteries? Be as specific as possible.

- If you could do anything for fun with no concern about the cost, what would you do?
- Describe your ideal two-week vacation (when, where, with whom, activities, and so on).
- Think about the people you know who are the most fun to be around. What makes them so much fun?
- Describe the most fun you've ever had.
- Explore Pinterest, Groupon, and Meetup.com and write a list of activities you'd like to try.
- Whenever you see someone doing something that makes you think, "Wow, that looks like fun," write it down.

Impress Your Idea of Fun on Your Subconscious Mind

Create a vision board (a collage) of all the fun activities you'd like to do. You may create it in a few hours or spend several weeks to months finding images. What's important is that the process of creating the board compels you to think about having fun.

Hang your vision board in a place where you'll see it every day, preferably several times daily. Your vision board will be a daily reminder to you to have more fun, and it will reinforce the idea of having fun, impressing that idea on your subconscious mind.

Watch YouTube or TikTok videos or cable TV shows of people having fun engaging in the activities you think you'd enjoy. Watching videos is an effective intermediate step between thinking about an activity and doing it. It feeds your imagination and elicits positive emotional responses while providing valuable how-to instruction. Pinterest and Instagram can be effective, as well.

As you feed your mind images of fun activities, repeat the following affirmation twice or three times daily with a smile on your face:

> I'm having more fun than a barrel of monkeys. I'm fun to be around and am surrounded by smart, exciting, and energetic people doing what I love to do in the place I want to be.

Make Dull Activities More Fun

You don't need to limit fun to special activities outside your daily routine. You can make every day more fun at home, school, work, and wherever else you spend your time. Here are a few suggestions for making even the most mundane activities more fun (you don't have to try them all, but try at least a few of them):

- **Tweak your routines.** Take a different route or mode of transportation to school or work. Eat something different for breakfast. Collaborate on a task you would normally do by yourself.
- **Listen to music in the morning.** If you tend to wake up in a bad mood or you have trouble getting out of bed, try listening to some upbeat music. Music can really get you revved up to start your day with positive energy.
- **Sing, dance.** Sing in the shower, dance while you're getting dressed.
- **Go people watching.** Spend a few hours downtown or at a popular park or a busy shopping mall or other location with lots of people and observe. Watching other people go about their lives can be entertaining. At the same time, it shifts your attention away from any problems or concerns you may have.

- **Do something odd in public.** When you're in a busy location, you're not the only one watching people; they're watching you. Do something unexpected. Recite a poem on your bus ride, dance in the park. If you have an audience, you'll make their day more fun too!

- **Strike up a conversation with a stranger.** If you're waiting in line at a coffee shop or sitting next to someone at a sporting event, say something. Most people just stare blankly ahead or at one another's shoes. By striking up a conversation, you completely change the dynamic and make the waiting more enjoyable.

- **Visit a new restaurant.** Instead of eating at your favorite restaurants, try something new.

- **Play a practical joke on a friend or family member.** If you have a strong relationship with someone who has a good sense of humor, play a practical joke on the person to make the day more fun and memorable for both of you. Stuff their car or school locker full of balloons, for example. (Be sure the joke will be fun for everyone—no mean jokes.)

- **Change your look.** Different clothes, shoes, hairstyle, or accessories can freshen your outlook on life and subtly change the way other people interact with you, which can be fun to observe.

- **Personalize your living spaces.** You can rearrange the furniture or change the decor. In some high schools, students are allowed to decorate their lockers, and seniors can paint their parking spaces. Just be sure to honor your school's rules and code of conduct.

- **Invite a friend or coworker along.** Sometimes just having someone else you like to spend time with join you in a routine task like walking your dog is enough to make it fun and exciting.

Describe what you did to make a routine task more fun and how it transformed the experience, both in terms of what happened and how it made you feel.

Fill Your Mind with Smiles and Laughter

A sure sign that someone is having fun is that they're smiling and laughing. I've noticed that people who don't smile or laugh enough are usually those who fill their minds with serious and sad thoughts. They spend too much time following the news and worrying and complaining about the state that the world is in, even when it has very little, if any, direct impact on their lives.

One way to have more fun in life and fill it with smiles and laughter is to stop feeding your mind negative material and start feeding it upbeat content.

Start by paying close attention to what your mind is consuming daily from various sources—people, news, TV shows, movies, music, video games, and so on. For at least a couple days, keep a record of what your mind is exposed to and how it makes you feel (happy, inspired, sad, angry, anxious, disappointed).

Work toward reducing your mind's consumption of content that leaves you feeling depressed, anxious, or angry and increasing its exposure to content that makes you smile and laugh. Here are some ideas for more comedic content:

- Funny movies
- Funny podcasts
- Television sitcoms
- Stand-up comedians
- Joke books
- Humorous books (ask your librarian or check them out online)

- Funny homemade videos online on sites such as YouTube and TikTok
- Comic strips

According to an adage attributed to various writers in the past, "Life is a tragedy to those who feel, and a comedy for those who think." As you increase your exposure to humor, your perspective begins to change. Humor enables you to transcend what might otherwise make you cry by laughing it off.

CHAPTER 14
Travel the World

Nothing develops intelligence like travel.
—EMILE ZOLA, FRENCH NOVELIST, JOURNALIST, AND PLAYWRIGHT

One of the best ways to expand your consciousness is to travel to unfamiliar places around the world and become immersed in cultures other than your own. Through travel, you're exposed to different environments, perspectives, values, and lifestyles while at the same time having the opportunity to view your own culture and beliefs from a distance.

Unfortunately, many of us become so comfortable and complacent in our current living situations that we lack the energy and initiative to explore unfamiliar locations. Or we're so afflicted with a fear of the unknown that we remain anchored in place, refusing to budge. As a result, we deny ourselves many of these benefits of world travel:

- Enhances creativity
- Improves communication skills
- Expands your perspective
- Boosts your confidence

- Increases your knowledge and understanding of the world and of yourself
- Enhances your enjoyment of life
- Improves your health
- Helps to discover your life's purpose
- Increases your appreciation of home
- Humbles you
- Improves your understanding and acceptance of others
- Increases your interconnectedness with others

If you haven't traveled outside your home country, I strongly encourage you to do so, especially when you're young. In your youth, you have fewer responsibilities to anchor you to any given place. Of course, you also have less money, but thanks to the power of your subconscious mind, travel expenses are never an insurmountable obstacle. In addition, there are always methods for making travel more affordable, such as taking advantage of study abroad programs or getting a job at your destination of choice. Wealthy relatives may be another option to explore. Just be sure not to let money concerns derail your travel plans—any concerns about money will drive it out of your life.

Choose a Destination

Before you can travel anywhere, you need to have a destination in mind. Where do you want to go?

If you have no idea, look at a world map. Better yet, hang a large world map in a prominent location in your bedroom or other suitable area of your home. In addition to providing inspiration for future trips, the map can serve as a record of places you've been and those you want to visit.

Another approach to sparking your imagination is to think about why you want to travel or what you plan to do when you get wherever it is you're going. Answer the following prompts to start thinking about the purpose of your trip:

- Are you looking more for adventure or relaxation? For example, camping and hiking in an Amazon jungle or hanging out on a beach? Be specific.
- Bustling metropolis or serene wilderness?
- Educational, cultural, just for fun, or all of the above?
- Work or play?
- Connecting with locals, traveling with friends/family, or both?
- What are your language preferences?
- What foods would you like to try?

Infinite intelligence, accessible through the power of your subconscious mind, can guide you in selecting the ideal destination for you. It knows what you like and what you need at this point in your life, and it knows everything about every location on the planet. Consult your subconscious mind for guidance by repeating the following affirmation several times daily:

Infinite intelligence knows who I am, what I need, and where I truly want to be at every moment of my life, and it reveals the ideal travel destination for me at this stage of my life.

The answer may come to you in a dream or as an inexplicable urge to visit a certain location. It may come to you as a suggestion from a friend or family member, something you see on TV or online or in a movie, a travel brochure that arrives in the mail, during a class at school, or in some other form. You can trust your subconscious mind to deliver the answer, but you cannot dictate how it delivers that answer.

Get Your Mind in the Game

As soon as you decide to travel somewhere, start planning your trip. The planning process will help to crystallize the mental image of your trip and impress it upon your subconscious mind, so that your subconscious can begin working out all the logistics. Here are some suggestions for getting both your conscious and subconscious minds in the game:

- Create a vision board for your desired destination. Include pictures of places you'd like to visit, the people of the area, the flora and fauna, activities you'd like to do there, and so on.
- Read stories/novels or watch movies set in your destination country.
- Explore modes of travel (how do you plan to get there and move around when you get there)? Think planes, trains, automobiles, buses, boats, and hiking.
- Research the destination. You can find plenty of information online and in traditional publications. Here's a short list of resources to check out:
  - Wikitravel at wikitravel.org
  - The World Factbook at www.cia.gov/the-world-factbook
  - YouTube videos
  - Travel podcasts
  - Travel blogs (search for the country followed by "blogs")

- Reddit's travel forums at www.reddit.com/r/travel
- Guidebooks, such as Frommer's, Lonely Planet, and Rough Guides
- Travel documentaries
- Travel magazines

- Check out different living arrangements, such as the following:
  - Couch surfing (sleeping for free or low cost at other people's houses)—you can find couch surfing opportunities on sites such as www.couchsurfing.com.
  - Hostels (low-cost, short-term social lodging)— traditional travel sites such as Expedia.com have info on hostels, or you can use a dedicated site such as HostelWorld.com.
  - Vacation rentals such as those available through Airbnb.com and Vrbo.com
  - Study abroad programs (in which you stay with a host family), which you can explore online at sites such as StudyAbroad.com—also look into intern abroad, volunteer abroad, teach abroad, and work abroad programs.
  - College—enroll in a college and stay in a dorm or off-campus housing.
  - Apartment (private or with a roommate)—you can find out more on sites such as Rentberry.com.

- Talk about your trip. Talking about it not only gets your mind engaged but also informs others who may be able to offer assistance—travel advice, people they know who live abroad, money, and so on.
- Obtain your passport. For details about obtaining a US passport, visit www.usa.gov/passport.

- If you're traveling to a country where you're unfamiliar with the language, start learning a few key words and phrases, such as *Hello, Please, Thank you, and My name is—*.
- Explore financial logistics (how you're going to get money from home and pay for stuff)—bank account, credit cards, debit cards, ATMs, e-payment platforms such as Xoom at www .xoom.com.
- Create a travel budget.
- Jot down a list of items to pack.

In addition to engaging your mind, each of these tasks brings you one step closer to taking the trip, so that when you get down to the nitty-gritty of actually planning your trip, it won't feel so overwhelming. What may start out looking like a huge leap becomes a short hop to departure.

Explore Your Hometown and Country

World travel is the ultimate goal, but you can find adventure and explore different foods and cultures within the confines of your hometown and country. Even relatively small towns have museums, historic sites, ethnic restaurants, sporting events, cultural festivals, concerts, parks, nature preserves, and more. Here are a few suggestions for expanding your consciousness through local travel:

- Set a goal to visit one new place in or near your hometown every week or at least once a month.
- Consult your town or county visitor's bureau to find out about local attractions, recreation, stores, restaurants, and events. Most towns or counties have websites; google your town or county name followed by "visitor bureau."

- If your town has a public transportation system, use it. Get a bus pass for the day and ride the bus with no destination in mind.
- Attend a local event, such as the farmers' market, a concert, or a festival. Don't overlook the local culture.
- Take long, meandering walks through your neighborhood. You never know what you'll discover.
- Visit a local museum, library, or historic site.
- Shop at an ethnic grocery store and strike up a conversation with someone who's working or shopping there.
- Head to the nearest body of water for a day of fishing, boating, or swimming.
- Visit a local park or nature preserve and spend a few hours exploring what it has to offer.
- Explore publicly accessible buildings, such as the county courthouse, town hall, library, and community center.

CHAPTER 15

Excel at School and Beyond

Develop a passion for learning. If you do,
you will never cease to grow.
— ANTHONY J. D'ANGELO, AUTHOR AND EDUCATOR

One of the biggest obstacles we face on our path to success in life is an impaired ability or willingness to learn. The root cause is often a lack of discipline and persistence, but it can also be a lack of interest, conflicting interests and commitments (no time), arrogance (we think we know everything), fear (we're afraid to try), lack of confidence (we think we're "just not good at something"), poor diet, poor sleep, or a host of other factors.

As humans, we can come up with all sorts of excuses for not learning, but what we can't do is blame it on our brains. The human brain is an amazing organ, and thanks to neuroplasticity, it's capable of learning and improving its own performance. Neuroplasticity involves the ability to grow new neurons and develop new neural pathways (connections between neurons).

Although we rarely give it much thought, as we learn, our brains are in a constant process of rewiring themselves, so the more we review and practice, the smarter we become, and the easier it becomes to perform a complex task, such as knitting a sweater, playing a musical instrument, or communicating in a foreign language.

Yes, learning something new requires some effort, but just as you must exercise to build muscle, your brain must put forth some effort to promote the development of neurons and neural pathways. Learning isn't always easy, but it is always rewarding.

They Said I'd Never Amount to Anything

I spoke with a thirty-two-year-old handyman who told me that at eighteen years old he had dropped out of high school. He said that he didn't do well in school because he was more interested in socializing and having fun and that several teachers told him that he "would never amount to anything."

At eighteen, he started his own tree-trimming business. He then worked in construction, framing and siding houses, installing roofs, hanging gutters, doing some light electrical and plumbing work, rehabbing kitchens and bathrooms, and so on. The only thing he said he wasn't skilled at was installing carpet. Over the course of fourteen years, he had developed into a fine craftsman, built a profitable business, started a family, and was pursuing his dream to move his family to Alaska and become a trapper. I believe he will achieve that dream.

This young man may have been a poor student in school, but he obviously had the potential to learn. All he lacked was motivation. As he faced the challenge of making a living and supporting his family, he found the motivation, the missing ingredient, and was on the highway to a successful and fulfilling life.

Self-Motivate for Success in School

I don't advise dropping out of school. What I do advise is that you find motivation to excel. Some teachers are very effective motivating students; some aren't. Don't rely on teachers to motivate you. Self-motivate. Nurture a sense of curiosity and fascination in yourself, and a love of learning.

I often hear students complain that they won't use what they're being taught later in life. They question the relevance of learning a foreign language, writing essays, or studying history or geometry. Learning never goes to waste. It strengthens the mind and provides it with valuable information and understanding for analyzing situations and problems from multiple perspectives. In addition, learning fuels creativity, enriches our minds, and expands our consciousness.

Try the following self-motivation techniques to optimize your academic performance:

- Prioritize learning and doing over grades. Understanding and retaining the subject matter will naturally result in high grades.
- Pay attention and participate in class. You'll get more out of it.
- Establish a study routine with fixed blocks of time devoted to study.
- Find or create a few study environments free from distractions. Then use them.
- Study in short spurts with intermittent breaks. You learn better when your mind is fresh, and breaks give your brain time to process the new information.
- Team up with a study partner or organize a study group.
- Reinforce what you're learning with outside sources. For example, if you're studying about the civil rights era in history class, read a book or watch a documentary about it.

- Engage in positive self-talk. If you're struggling in a class, for example, recite the following affirmation:

[Class or course name] is fascinating. I learn more about [subject] every day, and the more I learn, the easier it gets. I ask questions and seek help when necessary, and my teacher and fellow students are very supportive. I complete and submit all assignments on time, and I feel fully prepared for quizzes and exams.

What Do You Want to Learn Next?

Henry Ford once said, "Anyone who stops learning is old, whether at twenty or eighty. Anyone who keeps learning stays young." To remain young and vibrant, always be learning. Find a subject or skill that interests you, something you fall asleep thinking about and wake up with a hunger to learn, and then master it. It could be a school subject such as math or oceanography, an extracurricular activity like playing a musical instrument or acting, a skill such as carpentry or sewing, or any topic of interest you'd like to explore such as game theory. If you have a passion for a topic or a strong desire to develop a new skill, learning will come easy because you'll enjoy the work required.

Take some time to explore your interests by responding to the following prompts:

- What skill would you most like to have? For example, public speaking, carpentry, programming, cooking, windsurfing, knitting.
- What are you most curious about or fascinated with? What would you like to know more about? For example, human behavior, health/medicine, relationships, history, nature, UFOs.

- What's the most pressing problem you would solve if you knew how to solve it?
- If you could hire an expert to teach you something, what would that be?
- What would you like to know well enough to teach it?

Trust Your Subconscious Mind to Guide You

Imagine having a mentor guiding your educational and career decisions, someone who knows you intimately, is acting in your best interest, is familiar with your preferred learning style, and knows all the best sources for information and guidance. This imaginary mentor would be like a parent or high school guidance counselor but would know you far better, have a superior knowledge of available educational resources, and could attract those resources to you.

Well, you already have such a mentor—your subconscious mind. You just need to trust it and call on it for assistance.

Repeat the following affirmation several times daily:

Infinite intelligence knows me and knows what I need to know to live a prosperous, fulfilling, and exciting life. It guides me in my studies and brings people and other learning resources into my life at the appropriate times. I believe in myself and my abilities, and I easily learn anything that I set my mind to.

Ease into It

Learning may take time, but it needn't be difficult. In fact, the closer you get to mastering a subject or skill, the easier it becomes.

Some knowledge and expertise become so ingrained that eventually you reach a point at which these skills require little to no conscious effort to recall. The entire body of knowledge is transferred to the subconscious, and, through repetition, you develop muscle memory. You've already developed muscle memory for a number of skills, such as walking, talking, riding a bicycle, playing a sport, brushing your teeth, and so on.

As you review subject matter and practice a skill, your brain develops new neurons and neural pathways, so learning relies more on repetition than hard work. You don't have to learn everything or achieve mastery all at once. Trying to do so can make your learning seem overwhelming and obstacles to learning insurmountable. Study and practice regularly without expecting to learn everything you need to know in a single sitting.

Focus less on the goal and more on the process, spending a minimum time each day in study and practice. Trust your subconscious mind to build the neurons and neural networks necessary to hardwire the knowledge, understanding, and any muscle coordination necessary.

Remind yourself of the complex skills you now have that you developed gradually—crawling, walking, talking, riding a bike, writing. Does it feel as though you put forth some great effort developing those skills? Do you recall how much time and effort were required? I'm guessing not, because developing these skills wasn't difficult. They developed naturally and gradually through trial and error and lots of repetition.

Imagine learning anything just that easily. Now, convince your mind of it.

Sleep on It

In his youth, American clairvoyant Edgar Cayce, known as "the sleeping prophet," was struggling with spelling even the simplest words, like *cabin*. One night, he fell asleep on his spelling book. When he awoke, he knew how to spell every word in that book.

I'm not suggesting that learning is that easy. Nor do I recommend that you study calculus by putting your textbook under your pillow at night. I tell this story to make the point that sleep enhances learning. You can spend several hours studying a subject or trying to memorize a passage without making much progress and then sleep through the night and wake up knowing it perfectly.

Sleep enhances learning in two ways: One way is that during sleep the brain processes information and forms memories. The other way is that sleep suspends conscious thought, enabling the subconscious mind to deliver the knowledge and understanding.

If you're ever struggling with a subject or trying to memorize something, alternate periods of study with periods of sleep. Give your mind the time it needs to process the information.

Support Your Brain's Health and Function

Your brain is more powerful and adaptable than any supercomputer on the planet, but you need to care for it properly. To keep your brain in tip-top shape, follow these suggestions:

- Eat a balanced diet of mostly plant-based foods (vegetables, fruits, nuts, seeds, and healthy grains). Include healthy fats—the human brain is 60 percent fat. Omega-3 fatty acids found mostly in fish (especially salmon, sardines, herring, and anchovies) and some nuts and seeds (walnuts and chia seeds especially) are essential for brain health and function.

- Avoid consuming any foods or substances that harm the brain, such as sugar, aspartame, refined carbs, trans fats, highly processed foods, alcohol, marijuana, and illegal drugs.
- Get eight to ten hours of sleep per night. The brain detoxes itself primarily during sleep. Neglecting sleep takes a toll on it over time.
- Drink plenty of water during the day to support the body's detox pathways.
- Exercise regularly to promote healthy circulation to the brain. Alternate cardiovascular workouts with strength training for optimum results. Your brain needs oxygen. When blood flow is cut off to the brain, a person will lose consciousness in just ten seconds.
- Avoid emotional and psychological stress as much as possible. As you begin to rely on infinite intelligence to guide you in all ways, your life and your relationships with others will become more harmonious and peaceful.
- Stay mentally active. Read, write, solve problems or puzzles, play games, learn something new, socialize.
- Protect against head trauma. For example, wear a helmet when riding a bicycle or playing contact sports.

Although the mind transcends the body in many ways, the brain is a key component in the mind-body axis. It is what ultimately provides you with a vital connection to universal consciousness in this physical world. Take care of it and use it wisely. The most important freedoms you have are the freedom to think and the freedom to choose. Without a healthy, thriving brain, you place those freedoms at risk.

CHAPTER 16

Make the World a Better Place

*Successful people have a social responsibility to make
the world a better place and not just take from it.*
—CARRIE UNDERWOOD, RECORDING ARTIST

Our subconscious minds give us the power to make the world a
better place, and we have a responsibility to do just that. Imagine
any global challenge we currently face—poverty, disease, war, pollution, human rights. All these challenges are self-inflicted. They're
the products of distorted thoughts made manifest in the physical
world. They're created by humans who don't understand and appreciate the power of the subconscious mind and therefore use their
minds counterproductively. All problems, even very challenging
global problems, can be solved by humans, but the solutions require
a change of attitude.

The root cause of the world's most serious and persistent problems is *zero-sum thinking*—the false belief that a person can gain
something only if another person loses something of equal value.
In other words, for me to win, you need to lose. This false premise
creates deep-seated fear, which leads to selfishness and bigotry on
a small scale and poverty and war on a global scale. On the one

hand, zero-sum thinking encourages people to profit at the expense of others. On the other hand, it makes those susceptible to losing something feel as though they're living under the constant threat that someone will take away what's theirs.

The opposite of zero-sum thinking is innovation. Instead of profiting from someone's loss, you invent solutions that benefit not only you but others as well. Your innovations create wealth "out of thin air," enhancing people's lives and often providing opportunities for them to profit from your ideas. Just think of all the people who make a living off the ideas of innovators such as Steve Jobs (Apple), Elon Musk (Tesla), and Marissa Mayer (Google). Their innovations made them wealthy but also produced wealth for thousands, if not millions of others. And their innovations all began as seeds of thought sown into the fertile soil of the subconscious mind.

Look for Trouble

We say that someone who's trying to provoke an argument or fight is "looking for trouble," which is something not to be encouraged. However, when I advise you to look for trouble, I'm telling you to be sensitive to the problems people face. Most inventions are solutions to problems. Electric vehicles are a solution for problems such as pollution, climate change, and limited oil and gas supplies; mobile phones solve the problem of staying in touch when you're away from home; the mousetrap solves the problem of rodent infestations.

Take a few moments to think about the inventions that make your life easier or better. Make a top ten list, naming the invention and the problem it solves. (Keep in mind that an invention doesn't need to be a tangible object. It can be a service such as Spotify, an organization such as the Red Cross, a business model such as Costco, or any novel idea or creation.)

Carry around a small notebook and when you notice a problem for which there is no solution you know of, write a description of it. Then, research the problem online to see whether there is, in fact, an innovative solution. If you can't find a solution to the problem, you may have discovered a golden opportunity to invent a solution of your own that makes the world a better place and could make you quite wealthy.

Engage Your Imagination

Your conscious mind is rational. Your subconscious is creative. If you're struggling rationally to come up with a solution to a problem, engage your subconscious mind, instead. Begin at once to think constructively about the problem or challenge you face, confident that infinite intelligence has the solution. If you're worried, you're not confident. Confidence is the absence of fear and doubt.

Here are the steps of a simple technique you can use to receive guidance through the power of your subconscious mind:

1. Quiet your mind and still your body. Tell your body to relax; it must obey you.
2. Mobilize your attention; focus your thoughts on the solution to your problem.
3. Try to solve the problem with your conscious mind.
4. Think how happy you will be when you discover the solution. Imagine how you'll feel.
5. Let your mind play with this mood of happiness and content-ment in a relaxed way; then drop off to sleep.

6. When you wake up, if you don't have the answer, get busy with something else. While you're preoccupied with something else, the solution will pop into your mind.

Volunteer for a Cause

One of the best ways to engage your subconscious mind for the betterment of the world is to volunteer for a cause. When you actively participate in an organization with members who share your passion, you can't help but transfer your vision for a better tomorrow to your subconscious mind, which will work tirelessly to manifest that vision in the physical world. In addition, your thoughts unite with the thoughts of others in the group to raise awareness, through universal consciousness, about the problem and the need for a solution.

If you're not already supporting a cause with your time and talents, start thinking about a cause you could get passionate about. Here's a list of national and international organizations with youth volunteer programs that might help to spark your own ideas (you can google your town and state followed by "youth volunteer" to explore local opportunities):

- Earth Echo International (www.earthecho.org)
- Habitat for Humanity (www.habitat.org)
- American Red Cross (www.redcross.org)
- The United Nations (www.unv.org)
- The Humane Society (www.humanesociety.org)
- The Sierra Club (www.sierraclub.org)
- DoSomething.org (www.dosomething.org)

People who volunteer are happier, on average, than those who don't, which shouldn't be surprising given the many benefits of volunteering:

- Clear sense of purpose
- Expanded consciousness
- Membership in a community of people with shared values
- Opportunity to make new friends
- Improved social skills
- Enhanced self-esteem and confidence
- Free training to develop new skills
- Potential job leads and references
- Possible travel opportunities

Meditate

Over the course of history, especially during challenging times, world leaders have asked their people to pray for better times—for rain during long droughts, victory in war, unity amid division, peace in times of turmoil. There's a reason for that—prayer works. But it doesn't work the way many people think it does—with a divine being descending from the heavens to intervene in the lives of humans. It works by raising the collective consciousness of a large group of people who share the hope of a peaceful, prosperous future.

I don't like to use the word *prayer* because it's so misunderstood. Many people pray simply by asking the divine entity they believe in for what they want. Then, when they don't get it, they're disappointed. Worse, their faith is diminished as a result, making future prayer even less effective.

I prefer to use the word *meditate*, which emphasizes thought over words. To meditate is to think deeply or focus the mind on something for a period of time. While some people meditate to relax, it's also an effective way to transfer thoughts and emotions to the subconscious mind.

When you meditate for the purpose of making the world a better place, imagine the perfect world. I envision a world where its leaders collaborate to improve the lives of everyone and the overall condition of the planet, where everyone lives in peace and harmony, the oceans are clean and brimming with life, the land is blanketed in fields and forests teaming with fascinating creatures, the air is fresh and floral, and nature and technology are perfectly integrated—pretty much the fictional utopia of Wakanda, home of the Marvel Comics superhero Black Panther, or the utopian society depicted in the movie *Tomorrowland*. What does your utopia look like?

You can also choose to make your meditation more focused. For example, you can envision rainforests around the world being restored, your leaders in government being guided by infinite intelligence, a new technology that produces cheap energy, abundant harvests and distribution networks to ensure food security around the globe, rewarding work opportunities for everyone, and so on.

The key to successful meditation isn't simply to wish or ask for the world you desire. You must believe without a doubt that your subconscious mind, working through universal consciousness, is making your vision manifest in the physical world.

Recall from chapter 2 that thought must be infused with strong positive emotion to transfer it to your subconscious mind. As you create the mental image of your utopia, let your heart fill will joy, awe, and gratitude that your ideal world is coming to fruition in the physical world.

Reciting an affirmation can help infuse your mental image with strong positive emotion. Here's an example of an affirmation you can use:

> Infinite intelligence is creating the perfect world of abundance and incredible beauty. World leaders are inspired and dedicated to doing what is best and right. People around the world are living in peace and harmony with one another and with nature. Awesome technologies enrich our lives. It is a joy to be alive. I am filled with gratitude.

Write your own daily affirmation for making the world a better place and recite it to yourself several times daily.

Be Generous and Compassionate

One of the most effective ways to make the world a better place is to make yourself a better person—a person who's more generous, compassionate, and understanding. You may not be able to change people who are selfish and uncaring, but you can improve yourself, and any improvements you make will positively influence others by the example you set.

- Forgive others and yourself. Let go of any anger, bitterness, resentment, regret, or guilt.
- Find your center outside yourself—in people, activities, or a cause. Self-centered people tend to be selfish, close-minded, and unhappy.

- Be helpful. Look for ways to make life easier and more pleasant for the people in your life.
- Be polite. Saying "please" and "thank you" and treating people with respect and appreciation doesn't seem like a big thing, but it goes a long way toward building an environment of peace and harmony.
- Give freely. Donating time, talents, and riches not only feels good, but it also facilitates the free flow of abundance and wealth.

CHAPTER 17
Develop Your Psychic Powers

Discover the truth about your underlying psychic gifts and not only stop thinking of yourself as crazy but also empower yourself to make a major difference in the lives of others.
—Catherine Carrigan, Medical Intuitive Healer

Through your connection with universal consciousness, you have psychic powers—clairvoyance, clairaudience, astral projection, automatic writing, channeling, psychic healing, precognition, remote viewing, retrocognition, telekinesis, levitation, mental telepathy, and more. Shortly, I'll explain what each of these powers is. All that's preventing you from using them is a lack of knowledge and practice. You have the abilities but haven't yet developed them. This shouldn't be a big surprise; after all, everyone has the ability to play a musical instrument, but most of us haven't developed that ability.

You can see into the future, heal yourself and others, travel to remote locations without ever leaving the room you're sitting in, and more. You simply haven't developed those abilities.

Well, that's about to change. In this chapter, I describe various psychic abilities, explain how to use the power of your subconscious mind to develop them, and tell several stories of people who demonstrated these amazing abilities.

Recognizing Different Psychic Powers

We generally think of psychic powers only in the realm of science fiction and superheroes. Magneto from *X-Men* can manipulate mental objects with his mind. Cyclone, a Marvel Comics character, can control the wind. Doctor Strange is capable of astral projection and levitation. Mystique from *X-Men* can dematerialize and rematerialize. Stephen Jameson from *The Tomorrow People* can communicate telepathically. But psychic powers somewhat like those are available to all of us through universal consciousness, which permeates you and everything else in the universe. Anything that can be imagined in the mind is possible because everything is created first in consciousness, then in the physical world.

Here's a list of some of the more common psychic powers defined:

- **Astral projection** involves an out-of-body experience (OBE), in which a person's consciousness separates from the physical body to travel to remote locations.
- **Automatic writing** is the faculty of producing written insights and foresights without conscious intent.
- **Channeling** is the practice of acting as a medium through which the consciousness of other beings communicate.
- **Clairaudience** is the faculty of perceiving as if by hearing, an inaudible message; for example, "hearing" your mom warn you about something dangerous when she's a thousand miles away.
- **Clairvoyance** is the ability to perceive a person, object, or location through means other than the five senses; for example,

Abraham Lincoln is said to have viewed his own body lying in rest days before he was assassinated.

- **Levitation** is the action of rising or causing something to rise in the air. St. Joseph of Cupertino, the "flying saint" from the 1600s, was witnessed by many churchgoers to rise above the altar during mass on several occasions.
- **Mental telepathy** is the ability to communicate solely through thought, without the use of spoken words or physical gestures.
- **Psychic healing** involves curing illness and restoring health through the power of thought, with or without physical interventions such as medicine or surgery.
- **Remote viewing** is the ability to receive visions or mental impressions from a distant object or place. During the Cold War, the United States and Russia both experimented with remote viewing to spy on one another.
- **Retrocognition** is the ability to see or experience past events you had no previous knowledge of (for example, knowing about historical events or the lives of historical figures without ever having been exposed to any information about them).
- **Telekinesis** is the ability to move physical objects with the mind alone. The thought process alone is telekinetic, because it involves moving chemical and electrical messengers in your brain. And, as you learned in chapter 1, the physical movement of *anything* in the universe impacts *everything* in the universe.

Although these psychic powers are available to everyone through the functioning of the subconscious mind, some people are more psychic than others, and the specific power seems to vary among individuals. Psychic energy may manifest as clairvoyance in one person, astral projection in another, psychic healing in a third, and so forth.

Have you ever experienced or witnessed a psychic phenomenon? If so, briefly describe your experience or what you observed.

You Are Psychic

How often have you thought of a person and then heard the phone ring, and behold, you knew it was your friend calling? Or maybe you sensed that someone close to was in trouble and when you called that person you discovered that your intuitive sense was accurate.

You can develop those psychic abilities by making a conscious effort to engage your subconscious mind. Every night relax your body as follows, by affirming quietly:

> My toes are relaxed, my feet are relaxed, my ankles are relaxed, the calves of my legs are relaxed, my thighs are relaxed, my abdominal muscles are relaxed, my heart and lungs are relaxed, my neck is relaxed, my hands and arms are relaxed, my head is relaxed, my eyes are relaxed, my brain is relaxed, my whole being is relaxed, and I am at peace.

In this relaxed state, you can implant the following ideas in your subconscious mind effectively prior to sleep:

> Infinite Intelligence reveals to me everything I need to know at every moment of time and point of space. I am divinely inspired and divinely guided in all my ways. I intuitively perceive the truth about every situation. I hear truth, I see truth, I know truth. Divine love saturates my entire being. I am illu-

mined by the wisdom of infinite intelligence, and I have [names of psychic power(s) you desire]. The only voice I hear is the inner voice of infinite intelligence.

Remember that you are most receptive to psychic energy when conscious thought is suspended. Many people with psychic powers experience them only when in a trance or trance-like state—when they're lost in meditation. The secret is to reach a state of *not* thinking. Let your conscious self escape the prison of your physical body. In a state of pure consciousness, you can fully experience your psychic powers.

Caution: Be careful to use whatever psychic powers you have to bless, help, heal, and inspire. Never use these powers to take advantage of any person or to harm them in any way. To misuse the powers of your mind would cause a disastrous reaction in yourself because you are the only thinker in your universe, and your thought, being creative, will bring into your own life what you affirm or believe about the other person.

She Sensed Danger

A young nurse planned a plane trip, but the night before her scheduled departure, she had a vivid experience. In a dream, she saw the plane hijacked, and an inner voice spoke to her and said, "Cancel your trip." She awakened startled, but she followed the inner instruction and canceled the flight. She discovered later that the plane she had been scheduled to be on was hijacked.

The guiding principle of her subconscious caused her to see the event before it happened in order to protect her. The plan to hijack the plane was in universal consciousness long before the day of the scheduled flight. It was placed there via the subconscious minds of the terrorists who had planned it. Through the intuitive power of her own subconscious mind, she gained access to this universal consciousness to learn of the plan.

She was able to use her subconscious mind as an early warning system by repeating the following affirmation as she fell asleep each night:

Perfect love surrounds me wherever I go, making my journey safe, joyous, and peaceful. Infinite intelligence prepares my path and protects me. I lead a charmed life.

Through its connection with universal consciousness, the subconscious mind knows all, sees all, and responds to the nature of each person's thoughts. By repeating this affirmation every night, lovingly and with confidence and gratitude, she called on infinite intelligence to protect her, and it responded accordingly.

This Doctor Visited Patients with His Astral Body

Many people, consciously and unconsciously, have found themselves outside their natural bodies and have discovered that they have another body, sometimes called the subtle body, astral body, or fourth-dimensional body. It is a body with a higher molecular vibration, somewhat like a fan that oscillates at such a high speed that the blades become invisible. People can see, hear, and engage in extrasensory travel completely independent of their physical being.

American spiritual healer Phineas Parkhurst Quimby once said, "I know that I can condense my identity and appear also at a distance." His astral or fourth-dimensional body was as real to Dr.

Quimby as was his physical body, and these appearances of himself to patients 100 or more miles away from his home became routine for him. Time and time again, he demonstrated that humans are transcendental beings not bound by time, space, or matter.

In one instance, he wrote to a woman who lived a great distance from his home in Belfast, Maine, stating that he would visit her on a certain day, although he never revealed the exact time. Due to an oversight, the letter was never mailed. However, while the woman for whom he promised to visit was entertaining another woman at dinner, the guest said, "There is a man standing behind your chair," and she described him in detail. The lady of the house declared, "Oh, that is Dr. Quimby. He is treating me." Dr. Quimby was mentally and spiritually present with her, in his fourth-dimensional or subtle body, which was seen by the guest in the home.

Physically, Dr. Quimby was in his home in Belfast at that time, concentrating on his patient and contemplating the divine ideal—the healing, purifying force of the infinite healing presence flowing through his patient—and he decided at the same time to project himself into her presence, undoubtedly with the idea of instilling greater certainty in his patient that she would be healed.

Everything He Needed Came His Way

Robert Wright, nineteen years of age, assisted me every Saturday morning in putting together my radio program in a soundproof room in my home. He had been practicing the law of his mind every night before retiring by quietly exclaiming the following:

> Infinite intelligence in my subconscious mind guides me in all my studies in college and reveals to me all the answers. I am

always poised, serene, and calm, and I pass all my examinations in divine order. I know a car is an idea in universal mind, and I claim a new car now, which comes to me in divine order. I give thanks for the answered prayer. I know that the nature of my deeper mind is to respond to my requests, and I also know that my idea, when repeated faithfully, will be etched in my subconscious and come to pass.

The sequel was interesting. He experienced a pre-vision one night about a week prior to a special examination and saw all the questions to be asked. He subsequently got excellent marks and won a scholarship for a considerable sum of money, to aid him in his education. The car he was driving to college broke down on the freeway and, the same day, he was presented with a gift of a new car.

When the car broke down, he affirmed boldly: "Only good can come out of this," and only good came to him.

An Army Officer Hears His Brother's Voice: "You Will Be Saved"

Some years ago, I spoke at a club dinner, and an army officer sat next to me. He had just returned from Vietnam. He said that he and his brother had been wounded on patrol but that his brother died from the wounds before help could arrive. Then a very strange thing happened. The officer's brother appeared to him and said, "The medics are not far away; I will tell them where you are and you will be saved." In about half an hour, two medics arrived and administered aid to him. They said, "An officer appeared from nowhere and gave us specific directions." They described the officer and their description matched in every detail that of his departed brother. After a few hours the helicopter took him to an army hospital, where he recovered rapidly from his wounds.

There is really nothing strange about this when you stop and think things through. You are a mental and spiritual being. When you leave the body, you immediately assume your fourth-dimensional body. You can see and be seen, understand and be understood, and have a perfect memory. In other words, your personality never dies. The deceased brother had an intense desire to save his sibling's life. His subconscious mind knew the location of the medics and immediately projected himself there, enabling him to be seen by the medics. Also, his subconscious empowered him to speak and issue orders.

Today it is well known in scientific and academic laboratories that you can think, feel, see, hear, and travel, independent of your physical body. In other words, all the faculties of your senses can be duplicated in mind alone. Infinite Intelligence makes no mistakes, and it was, therefore, intended that you use all these faculties transcendentally of your physical body and environment. The subtle body, or the fourth-dimensional body, can appear and disappear at will, enter closed doors, give messages, move substantial objects. Remember, you will have bodies to infinity. These bodies are vibrating at a higher molecular frequency, more like fields of energy than physical objects.

An Out-of-Body Experience

A woman once told me that on one eventful Christmas Eve she had felt an intense desire to be with her mother in New York City. As she fell asleep, focusing all her thoughts on her former home in New

York City, she immediately found herself in her mother's home trying to open the front door. She managed to enter the back door, however, and went upstairs to her mother's room where her mother was lying awake in bed reading the paper.

Her mother was startled and asked, "Why didn't you let me know you were coming? I heard you come up the stairs; I knew it was you."

This woman kissed her mother and said, "Merry Christmas, Mom. I have to leave now," and she found herself back in her body in Los Angeles. She was able to describe everything in the room, and she had heard the Christmas carols on the radio clearly.

This is not an unusual experience. She was focused on her mother prior to sleep and had developed an intense desire to be with her on Christmas Eve. This desire charged her subconscious mind with a mission, and it projected her personality in a new body 3,000 miles away. Her mother experienced the touch of her lips and hands and heard her voice clearly. She entered through the back door even though it was locked and sat on a chair by her mother's bed. She was conscious of being out of her body and was aware of a more spirit-like body that could pass through locked doors or other material objects.

Fearlessly Experience This Awesome Universe

The universe is physical and metaphysical. The physical world is what we can see, feel, and touch. It is energy and matter. The metaphysical, which is no less real, is the awareness and intelligence that organizes, guides, and directs. It is consciousness, which flows through and encompasses everything in the physical universe and beyond.

Likewise, you are a physical and metaphysical being. Through your physical body, you are part of the physical universe and can fully experience physical reality. Through your metaphysical self, you are part of the metaphysical universe, part of the force that flows through and encompasses all. Your metaphysical self organizes, guides, and directs. It is a creative force, and it equips you with amazing psychic powers that transcend the physical realm while also enabling you to create your own reality within the physical realm.

Most people live only half their lives. They live totally in the physical realm, bound by their physical limitations and at the mercy of their circumstances. Don't settle for living only half your life. Engage your subconscious mind, which is your key to fully and fearlessly experiencing this awesome universe in both its physical and metaphysical majesty!

NEXT STEPS

Engaging the power of your subconscious mind to achieve success in all areas of your life requires a persistent and mindful approach. Slipping back into old habits and self-defeating or self-limiting thoughts is easy and far too common. Every minute of every day remain vigilant for any negative thoughts or ideas you may be exposed to.

Negative thoughts and ideas are often very subtle—for example, advertisements on television or social media for medications can plant seeds in your mind of illness, or someone can make a comment or ask a question that causes you to question or doubt your ability to achieve a goal. Remain vigilant and reject or at least challenge all negative, self-limiting thoughts. Counter all negative thoughts with positive affirmations and mental images.

Avoid negative people when possible. Debbie or Danny Downer will always focus on lack and limitation and try to drag people into the same hole they're in. Distance yourself from these people. If you cannot avoid them, or you want to help them, challenge their negativity. Offer solutions to their problems or challenge them to offer solutions of their own. If they're criticizing the way someone is handling a situation, for example, ask them what they would do differently or what they could do to help. If they're complaining about a rule they disagree with at school or work, ask them to explain why they disagree with it or how they could go about changing it.

Keep in mind that most negative thinking is over a situation that can be resolved or a problem that can be solved. Lack of insight and imagination is usually all that's standing in the way of a solution. Through the power of your subconscious mind, every problem can be solved.

Finally, don't set this book down never to read it again. Reread it every few months or whenever you start to feel frustrated or discouraged. This book can serve as a constant reminder that through the power of your subconscious mind, you hold the keys to your success. As long as you have the freedom to think, you have the power to be, do, and have whatever you put your mind to because everything you do, everything you achieve, and everything you create begins with a thought.

Change your thinking, change your life.

ABOUT THE AUTHOR

A native of Ireland who resettled in the United States, Joseph Murphy (1898–1981) was a Divine Science minister and author with a broad background in science, philosophy, psychology, religion, and mysticism. Over the course of his life, he studied the world's major religions, including Buddhism, Christianity, Hinduism, Judaism, and Islam, along with various divination systems, such as I Ching and Tarot cards.

Through his studies, experience, and interactions with others, Dr. Murphy recognized a common theme—that we are not victims of circumstance. To the contrary, we have the power to create our own reality and define our own destiny. He devoted his life to spreading this truth in an effort to empower as many people as possible to live rich and fulfilling lives.

A popular speaker, Dr. Murphy lectured on both American coasts and in Europe, Asia, and South Africa as Minister-Director of the Church of Divine Science in Los Angeles. His lectures and sermons were attended by thousands of people every Sunday. Millions of people listened to his daily radio program and read the over thirty books and countless pamphlets he has written.

He has been acclaimed as a major figure in the human potential movement; spiritual heir to writers like James Allen, Dale Carnegie, Napoleon Hill, and Norman Vincent Peale; and inspiration to contemporary motivational writers and speakers including Tony Robbins, Zig Ziglar, Louise Hay, and Earl Nightingale. He was one of the best-selling authors in the mid-twentieth century.

His book *The Power of Your Subconscious Mind* has sold millions of copies and has been translated into seventeen languages. It has never been out of print and is still one of the best sellers in the self-help genre.

Over the years Dr. Murphy gave lectures and radio talks to audiences all over the world. In his lectures he pointed out how real people have radically improved their lives by applying his unique techniques for fully engaging their subconscious minds to be, do, and have everything they want.